Speaking & Social Interaction

Speaking & Social Interaction

Second Edition

Susan M. Reinhart and Ira Fisher

Ann Arbor

THE UNIVERSITY OF MICHIGAN PRESS

Acknowledgments

The authors would like to thank the following people for their help in the preparation of the first edition of this textbook: Shirley Thompson of Georgetown University for her contribution to the unit on "Offers of help and requests for help"; Ann Borkin, who made a major contribution to the unit "Excuse me and I'm sorry"; Beth Eisler for her advice during the first stages of writing; Robin Scarcella of the University of California at Irvine and Jose Sanchez-H., without whose encouragement this text may not have been completed; Carolyn Madden of the University of Michigan for her useful comments on parts of the text; and Margaret Reinhart for proofreading the first manuscript. The authors are especially indebted to Cameron Beatty for his very careful and insightful review of the original manuscript and Margo Czinski for the many hours of help she gave us in revising the first manuscript. Their contribution was invaluable.

We wish to thank Christine Feak for her advice on revising the second edition of the text and Deborah Avelar for her assistance in preparing the manuscript. We are also very grateful to our editor at the University of Michigan Press, Kelly Sippell, for her patience and encouragement and to the anonymous reviewers who provided us with many useful recommendations for revising the original manuscript.

Photography credits

The authors especially wish to thank José Sánchez-H., California State University at Long Beach, and Gregory Fox, Gregory Fox Photography (Ann Arbor, Michigan) for their assistance in making the photographs. We are also grateful to the following people for their cooperation.

Kristen L. Behrendt	Cristina Fierro
Caroline Reinhart	Jenelle Harmon
Andrew S. Watson	Duy Nguyen
Yvonne Wyborne	Maria Moreno
Steve Caday	David Dunkin

Other
Speech Skills

* Turntaking
* Body language
* Checking for listener
  comprehension.

Authentic Communicative sit.
Reflection important
report back!

IDEAS

* Give sample sentences
  task stud. to identify function
  eg. Go two miles north
  then turn left at the
  lights.

Contents

Introduction

Speaking & Social Interaction was written for intermediate and advanced students of English as a second language. It consists of nine units that are meant to guide learners to use English as a tool for social interaction. *Speaking & Social Interaction* not only teaches important aspects of social interaction but also provides a framework for conversational analysis and practice. It deals with the appropriate use of English in a variety of social situations including making acquaintances, telephoning, giving opinions, agreeing and disagreeing, getting and giving advice, making invitations, and offering and requesting help.

Materials developed for *Speaking & Social Interaction* are based on the results of questionnaires by both native and nonnative speakers, discussions with and observations of native speakers of English from the United States, and the authors' own professional and personal experience.

Speaking & Social Interaction can be used either as the main or supplementary text in a speaking, culture, or language-in-use class or as a supplementary text in a skill-integrated classroom situation. Programming of the book is flexible. Units need not be used sequentially, nor does one unit need to be taught immediately after the previous unit has been completed. It is recommended, however, that the first unit be used during the first few days of class.

Speaking & Social Interaction can be used both in the United States and abroad with intermediate and advanced students of English. If used abroad, it is especially helpful for those students who have contact with Americans in their own countries and/or who are planning to visit or study in the United States.

Each unit consists of a warm-up, a dialogue or dialogues for analysis, expressions for use (when appropriate), points to remember, activities to be done by the class as a whole or in pairs or small groups, a community activity, a homework activity, and a final activity.

Warm-up. The Warm-up serves as an introduction to the material covered in the unit. It stimulates interest in the particular topic as well as motivates students to think about their own beliefs and practices in regard to a particular social situation.

Dialogue(s) for Analysis. The Dialogue(s) for Analysis section consists of a dialogue or dialogues followed by questions for discussion. These dialogues serve to introduce a specific social interaction for students to analyze and discuss. Discussion questions are concerned with such points as how the conversation began, the relationship between the two speakers and their feelings toward each other, the function of certain expressions in the dialogue, and potentially inappropriate use of the language. A tape accompanies this section.

Expressions Used. Several units in the text include lists of expressions. These lists are not meant to be memorized but to serve as reference material for students.

Points to Remember. Points to Remember summarizes the points that have been discussed in connection with the unit topic. These points are stated as rules of social interaction and are to be regarded as generally useful in the particular social situation being discussed.

Class Activity. The Class Activity is meant to be done with the class as a whole under the instructor's supervision. The activity may involve such activities as general discussion, the development of a role-play, or the correction of inappropriate or incorrect expressions. Depending on the size and level of the class, the instructor may prefer that students do this activity in small groups or pairs.

Pair and Small Group Activities. Pair and Small Group Activities generally consist of activities that are more appropriately done in small groups. These activities include role-plays, problem-solving discussions, and tasks to be completed. Role-plays are meant to be first discussed by the participants and then practiced and presented to the group or the class as a whole. Instructors can assign all the role-plays or only those they find most beneficial to their particular class.

Community Activity. The Community Activity is meant to encourage students to (1) observe the behavior of native speakers of English, (2) get information and opinions from Americans on various topics, and (3) think about and discuss cultural differences between the United States and their own country. Although this section is more easily carried out when students are living in the United States, instructors abroad may also be able to successfully use the majority of the community activities.

Homework Activity. The Homework Activity is designed to give students further opportunity to synthesize what they have learned in the unit and to work independently on a task. It also provides the instructor the opportunity to evaluate student progress and provide individual feedback.

Final Activity. The Final Activity provides a final opportunity for students to practice what they have learned in the unit. It also gives the instructor the opportunity to check for any misunderstandings or review problem areas students may still have. In addition, the final activity provides closure to the unit.

Each section of each unit includes instructions to the instructor. In addition, notes to the instructor provide a number of suggestions for using the text.

Notes to the Instructor

It is the intention of the authors that *Speaking & Social Interaction* be used in ways that are best suited to the needs of individual instructors and their classes. Thus, this section endeavors to discuss several approaches to sections of a typical unit. However, part of the success of speaking and social interaction depends on each instructor's assessment of his/her own situation and ability not only to experiment with suggestions we provide but also to contribute others.

Warm-up. The purpose of the Warm-up is to serve as an introduction to the unit. Unlike other sections, it is not meant to "teach" but rather to stimulate interest in the topic and motivate students to think briefly about their own and others' practices in regard to a particular social situation. Instructors generally pose warm-up questions orally to the class as a whole. The warm-up is meant to be short; in some cases, all questions need not be asked. In addition, instructors are encouraged to substitute questions that they think may be more suitable for their particular class.

In place of, or in addition to, a warm-up, an instructor may wish to write on the blackboard two or three questions that are answered in the lesson; for example, "What can you say if you want to extend an informal dinner invitation to a friend?" The point of this activity is not to discuss the answers to these questions but to give students an idea of what they can expect to learn from the unit. At the end of the unit the instructor can return to these questions for discussion and summary.

Dialogue(s) for Analysis. The Dialogue(s) for Analysis section consists of a dialogue or series of dialogues followed by discussion questions. The tape that accompanies the text contains the dialogue but not the discussion questions. More advanced students can listen to and discuss the dialogue without having to open their books. Intermediate students at some point may wish to follow along in their books. However, it should be kept in mind that the point of this section is *not* to provide listening practice to the students. Its main purpose is to introduce a specific social interaction for students to analyze and discuss.

The dialogues are meant to reflect as closely as possible a natural conversation between two speakers. The questions that follow focus on such points as how the conversation began, the relation between the two speakers, the function of the language used in the dialogue, the outcome of the conversation, and possible motives of the speakers.

Before the students begin listening to the tape, the instructor can introduce the characters and set up the situation verbally. Students will follow the conversation better if they have an idea of what to listen for.

Students may have questions about the vocabulary. These should be answered quickly. Too much time spent on vocabulary will detract from the focus of the section.

Each dialogue is followed by questions for discussion. However, in some units, there are a considerable number of questions based on one dialogue. It is important for instructors to use these questions as a guide for fruitful discussion, but it is not necessary to ask each question in sequence. Students should also be encouraged to analyze the dialogue on their own.

Instructors may wish to vary this section by having students work in small groups or by themselves. Conclusions about the dialogue, however, should then be made by the class as a whole.

Some instructors may feel that in certain units there are too many dialogues in the Dialogue(s) for Analysis Section. One suggestion is to begin by having students act out and discuss several role-plays found in the class activities. After discussing the role-plays, the instructor can, if necessary, return to one or more of the Dialogue(s) for Analysis Section. Otherwise, he/she can go on to discuss the Points to Remember.

Some instructors, on the other hand, may feel a certain amount of frustration that the dialogues don't give the students all or mostly all the information they need to know about the topic under discussion. They may think that students are somewhat unprepared to do some of the activities in the unit. However, it should be kept in mind that by expanding the use of dialogues in this section, we would run the risk of (1) including dialogues that sound repetitive or unnatural and (2) slowing down the pace of the class and losing student interest. We have, therefore, chosen to provide students with further information in other sections of the unit, particularly in Expressions for Use and Points to Remember. In addition, sections, such as Class Activity and Community Activity call on teachers and native speaker informants to provide information to the students that is not found in the text.

Expressions Used to . . . . Expressions Used provides students with a reference list of expressions that generally share the same function but may vary in terms of formality, impact, etc. The main purpose of this section is to introduce students to expressions they may not know and to briefly point out that the context and relationship between the speakers is relevant in choosing a particular expression.

Although part of the goal of this text is for students to expand their repertoire of expressions by trying them out in conversation, it is important to note that nonnative speakers of English, like native speakers, may prefer to use certain expressions rather than others. We feel that appropriate use and passive understanding of expressions is more important than attempts to use all the expressions.

The list of expressions should be discussed briefly and thereafter referred to as needed. Students can be encouraged to use the list when preparing their role-plays.

Points to Remember. Points to Remember is a summary of rules of interaction for the particular social situation being discussed in the unit. These rules serve only as a general guide, and the instructor may wish to expand or modify them for a particular region, social or age group, etc.

Points to Remember can be presented in lecture form by the instructor, or students can read the points and present them to the class. Students can also create their own points to remember and compare them to those in the book.

Class Activities done by the class as a whole are generally meant to be teacher-guided. In some of these activities, students are asked to correct inappropriate or incorrect expressions. These activities are based on nonnative speaker responses to questionnaires and thus may parallel responses that your students choose when interacting socially in English.

Pair and Group Activities. In this section students work on a role-play or other activity in pairs or small groups. Meanwhile, the instructor acts as a resource person or works with a particular group of students. If the class is small, all groups or group representatives may have the opportunity to present their work to the class. If not, groups can take turns during the semester. Class discussion and comments from students are encouraged during this section. Teachers are encouraged to substitute the role-plays in the text with others more suited to their particular class.

Students may initially feel uncomfortable about presenting their role-plays to the class. Peer and instructor feedback should be carried out in a way that will encourage discussion rather than criticism. The class and instructor can call attention to useful strategies of social interaction that students have adopted and in some cases suggest more socially appropriate expressions. Instructors can point out language strategies they themselves depend on in similar circumstances. The class can also discuss ways in which cultural differences may cause misunderstanding and what the speakers did or could have done to remedy this. In addition, instructors can help students who are overly concerned with correcting grammar to focus more on the social functions of language.

Community Activity. The Community Activity is an important but difficult section of the text. It is important because it gives students a chance to interview Americans, observe their behavior, and compare it to their own. It is a difficult section because sometimes students are reluctant to approach native speakers of English. The following suggestions may be helpful when assigning the community activity. First, students can be assigned the community activity on the first day of the unit and be given two to three days to finish it. Second, students can be allowed to interview in pairs for the first few units. Third, names and telephone numbers or addresses of native speakers who are willing to be interviewed can be handed out to the students. Fourth, if students are having trouble finding informants, informants can be brought to class or the instructor can serve as an informant.

This text focuses on American patterns of social interactions but can be adapted for use in Canada and possibly other English-speaking countries. The authors do not pretend to be experts on similarities and differences in Canadian and American styles of social interaction but feel that customs between the two countries are similar enough to make the text a worthwhile choice in Canada. Canadian instructors may need to rewrite instructions to the Community Activities, add or change several Points to Remember, and act as an informant for students. Canadian institutions can generally replace American ones.

If the book is used in non-English speaking countries abroad, students may know native speakers they can interview. Also, there may be several native speaker instructors willing to serve as informants either informally or in a short classroom interview. Videotapes can be made of these informants for future use. If there are no native speaker informants in the area, the instructor and students can elicit help from friends in the United States by asking them to write answers to the questions in an e-mail message or letter sent to the class. The students can discuss and compare information found in different responses. These same answers can be used with a new group of students.

As students begin to collect and compare information, they will realize that rules of social interaction in the United States are not necessarily clear-cut, which may also be the case in their own country. In addition, they may notice that certain aspects of social interaction vary from one area to another. Follow-up discussion and activities allow students to share their interview findings with other members of the class.

Homework Activity. The Homework Activity is provided to give students an opportunity to use what they have learned in the unit and to complete a task on their own. Homework is helpful in evaluating students' understanding of a particular unit and giving individual feedback. Homework and community activities are best assigned to be due on different days unless the class only meets once or twice a week.

Final Activity. The Final Activity provides a final opportunity for students to synthesize what they have learned. If students have successfully completed the other activities in the text and time is short, the final activity can be omitted. Many of the final activities are role-plays. Instructors are welcome to custom tailor these role-plays to their particular class. The number and type of role-plays assigned may depend on the enthusiasm of the students. If students feel role-plays are useful as well as fun, they will be more eager to participate in them. Feedback from the instructor as well as other students is therefore important. Many teachers find that video- and audiotape recordings of role-plays are extremely helpful in providing instructor and peer feedback. In addition, recordings encourage self-evaluation. They also serve as a record of students' progress throughout the semester. Native speakers can also be videotaped performing some of the final activities and their dialogues can be discussed and compared with those of the students. If the course also focuses on other speaking skills, such as pronunciation and increased fluency and vocabulary, student videotapes can provide opportunities for instructors to work with students on these skills to further improve effective communication.

It is our hope that teaching from *Speaking & Social Interaction* will be an enjoyable experience for you. If you have any comments about the text, we would appreciate hearing from you.

1

Making New Acquaintances and Informal Introductions

 Warm-up

1. Would you start a conversation with a person you didn't know? What would motivate you to talk to a stranger?

2. Can you think of a conversation you recently began with a stranger? Where were you? What was the reason? What did you talk about?

3. If you were sitting at a counter in a crowded restaurant, how might you begin a conversation with the person sitting next to you?

4. Under what circumstances would you introduce yourself to a person you struck up (started) a casual conversation with?

Dialogues for Analysis

Slow Service

Dialogue 1

Situation: Two foreign students, Yuji and Maria, are sitting at a counter in a restaurant waiting to be served. They have never met. Yuji is an 18-year-old student from Japan. He came to the United States to study English for six months and then will return to his country. Maria is a 19-year-old student from Venezuela. She'll study English for four more months and then go to Indiana University to study engineering. After a few minutes, one student turns to the other and speaks.

Maria: The service is really slow here. I've been trying to get the waiter's attention for the last ten minutes.

Yuji: I hope he waits on us soon. I've got a class at two.

Maria: Me, too. I recognize that English book. You must be a student at the English Language Center.

Yuji: Yeah. I'm in the fourth course. Are you studying there?

Maria: Yes. I'm in the fifth course. I finished the fourth course last month.

Yuji: I just came here two weeks ago. How do you like the institute?

Maria: It's pretty good. I think I've learned a lot of English so far.

Yuji: Yeah. I only wish the classes were a little smaller, though, because we don't get enough chance to talk. But I like my teachers a lot.

Maria: How long are you going to be here?

Yuji: I guess six months, but sometimes it seems so different here that I feel like going home tomorrow. And I really miss my family.

Maria: Yeah, it's hard at first, but you'll get used to it. Where are you from?

Yuji: Japan. How about you?

Maria: Venezuela. I'm only staying here four more months. Then I go to Indiana University.

Yuji: By the way, my name's Yuji.

Maria: Hi, I'm Maria.

Yuji: Pleased to meet you.

Maria: Nice to meet you, too.

Yuji: Oh, here comes the waiter. It looks like we're going to get served after all.

Maria: Good. I'm starving.

Dialogue Analysis

1. What situation leads up to the opening of the conversation between Maria and Yuji?

2. Does Maria start the conversation by introducing herself?

3. What does she say to start the conversation?

4. How does Yuji show he's interested in talking to Maria?

5. What other things do they talk about before telling each other their names?

6. What expression does Yuji use to casually introduce himself?

7. Why doesn't Yuji ask Maria her age?

8. Would you start a conversation with someone at a counter in a restaurant? In what situations do you feel comfortable talking to strangers? In what situations don't you feel comfortable talking to strangers?

Introducing a Friend

Dialogue 2

Situation: Maria and Yuji are eating their lunch when a friend of Maria's, Tom, comes up.

Tom:	Hi, Maria.
Maria:	Oh hi, Tom! Do you want to join us?
Tom:	Sure.
Maria:	Yuji, this is my friend, Tom. He lives in the apartment across from mine.
Tom:	Hi, Yuji. Nice to meet you.
Yuji:	Nice to meet you, too.
Maria:	Yuji's from Japan. He's studying at the English Language Center.
Tom:	How long have you been in the United States?

Dialogue Analysis

1. Maria not only introduces Tom and Yuji, but she also gives information about each of them. Why is that helpful?

2. What expression does Tom use when he is introduced to Yuji? How does Yuji respond?

3. What might give you the impression that Tom is a friendly person?

4. If Tom were just passing by, do you think Maria would still introduce him to Yuji?

▶ Points to Remember

1. Introduce yourself casually in informal situations. As the conversation develops, a simple introduction, such as "By the way, my name is . . . " or "I'm . . . , by the way" is generally considered sufficient.
2. If a friend comes along and stops to talk, informally introduce him/her to the person you are talking to. It is helpful to provide some information about each of them so that each will *(a)* know what your relationship is to the other person (friend, neighbor, wife, brother, instructor) and *(b)* have some information with which to begin a conversation.
3. When we are introduced to someone informally, we usually respond with "Nice/pleased to meet you" or "Hi, how are you?" "How do you do?" might be used in more formal situations and the response to this expression is generally "How do you do?"
4. Depending on the context, when you first meet a stranger, it may be inappropriate to talk about certain things such as salary, age, religion, or the value of someone's belongings.
5. In a number of student, work, and social environments, speaking to strangers can be enjoyable and lead to friendships. However, before talking to a stranger, assess your situation. If you are in a place where you do not feel comfortable speaking to a stranger, you are generally not required to do so.

Class Activity (to be done by the class as a whole)

Imagine you are on a plane flying to New York. You are sitting next to someone your age. First, think of three or four topics of conversation that would be appropriate to discuss with this person. Make a list of them with your class.

Example: "Have you been to New York before?"

- _____

- _____

- _____

- _____

Then, discuss

1. how you might begin the conversation,
2. under what circumstances you might introduce yourself, and
3. under what circumstances you might not want to start a conversation.

Class Activity (role-play in pairs)

Your teacher will team you with another student whom you may not know well and assign the following role-play:

On the first day you come early to your English class and begin a conversation with a student you don't know. Find out such things as:

- where the other person is from
- how long he/she has been studying English
- why he/she is taking English
- what he/she knows about the school or the class
- what he/she is going to do after finishing the English program

-

-

Then casually introduce yourselves and continue talking about things that you have in common.

Discuss with the class:

1. What were some of the topics you talked about?

2. What did you and the person you were talking to have in common?

3. How did you introduce yourselves? What did you say?

4. Do you think it would be harder to begin a conversation with an American in a classroom situation? Why or why not?

Homework Activity

In the following situations would you start a conversation with someone you didn't know? If not, explain why not. If so, write an opening to the conversation. Keep in mind the different locations and circumstances. Write your answers on a separate piece of paper. Be prepared to discuss your homework with others in the class.

1. You are waiting to see a professor. There is another student waiting to see her too. You are new at the university and don't know anything about the professor or the department. You haven't met many other students yet.
2. You are at a wedding of a friend. You came alone to the wedding. You are standing next to the food table. An older person whom you don't know is standing there, too.
3. You are a new member of the hiking club. You go to your first meeting and sit next to someone you don't know. The meeting won't begin for about five or ten minutes.
4. You are sitting downtown on a bench waiting for the city bus. You have about five minutes to wait before your bus comes. A man your age comes and sits down next to you. You have seen him on the bus before but haven't talked to him.

Community Activity

Do one of the following community activities outside of class. The purpose of these activities is for you to talk to American native speakers of English or to observe their behavior. You may also interview a native speaker of English from another country. With your class, discuss interesting differences in social customs you observed.

1. Find out the following information from an American. Bring your findings to class and compare them to both the information the other students collected and what you have learned in this unit.

   a. Have you recently struck up a conversation with someone you didn't know? What were the circumstances? Do you remember how you started the conversation?

   b. If you casually introduce yourself to another person, such as in class, in your neighborhood, at a social function, or at your work, would you shake hands?

   c. If you were sitting down and someone introduced you to a friend of his, under what circumstances would you stand up?

   d. Do you ever use the expression, "How do you do"? When might you use it? What might you say instead?

   e. Where would you be likely to begin a conversation with someone you didn't know? (*Note to student interviewer:* You may wish to name some locations if the person has trouble answering this question.)

   f. How might you strike up a conversation with someone sitting next to you on an airplane?

2. Listen to two Americans introducing themselves. Try and write down their dialogue as accurately as possible. Was the introduction similar to or different from the one between Maria and Yuji? Share your dialogue with other members of the class.

Notes

Final Activity (role-play in groups of threes)

Your teacher will group you with two other students and assign the following role play for you to prepare. First, discuss the role play with your group. Talk about how you will begin the conversation. List additional topics that you have in common and may want to discuss. Be prepared to perform the role play in front of the class. The instructor and the other students will discuss and compare each role play and make comments on how it can be improved.

You are at a farewell party for your friend Victor, who is moving to another city. You begin talking to the person sitting next to you. Make a list of the topics of conversation you can discuss. Talk about such things as:

• how you both met Victor

• what you both do

•

•

•

•

A friend comes over to talk to you. Introduce your friend to the person you just met and give information about them both. Continue discussing things you all have in common.

Notes

2

Using Questions to Get Specific Information and to Carry on a Conversation

Part One: Using Questions to Get Specific Information

 ## Warm-up

1. If you were thinking about taking a trip to Disney World, what information would you want to find out?

2. Where would be the best place to find out this information?

3. If you were at a party and were introduced to a woman who had just come back from a trip to India, what questions would you ask her? If you weren't planning to go to India, why would you ask her questions about her trip?

4. What are some reasons we ask questions?

Dialogue for Analysis

Planning a Trip to Japan

Situation: Karl is thinking about taking a trip to Japan this summer. In order to get information he needs, he goes to a travel agent.

Karl: I'm planning a trip to Japan this summer and was wondering if you could give me some information.

Agent: Sure.

Karl: How much is a round-trip flight leaving about July 1st?

Agent: Let's see. The cheapest one we have is $1,510. It's a direct flight leaving at noon.

Karl: Do you have any special packages that would include the flight, hotel, and food? I'd like to be there for about two or three weeks.

Agent: It looks like there's a two-week package for about $3,500. That includes hotel, transportation to and from the airport, and one day-long tour, but no meals.

Karl: Does it include a car?

Agent: No, but you could rent one.

Karl: How much does it cost? Or, is it easy to take local transportation?

Dialogue Analysis

1. What questions does Karl ask to get the information about traveling to Japan?

2. What other information might Karl need to know from the travel agent? What questions would he ask to get the information?

Class Activity (to be done by the class as a whole or in small groups)

You want to go to the American consulate in your country to get information about coming to the United States as a tourist. First, discuss some of the differences between coming to the United States as a tourist and coming as a student. Then, decide what questions you would ask to find out information you think you need to know.

 Class Activity (work in pairs)

Together with a partner, think of a city not far from where you are living that you would like to visit for a day or weekend (think of a place you might actually like to visit). You need to get information in order to plan your trip, such as how far away the city is, whether the bus or train goes there, and what interesting sights the city has. First, make a list of four or five questions you would ask. Then, make a list of the places (or people) you would contact to find out answers to the questions. If you don't know, ask your teacher or other students in the class for help. The telephone book is also a good source of information. Compare your list with the lists of other class members to see how they are similar or different.

Questions:

-
-
-
-
-

Places and people to contact

-
-
-

Community Activity

Do one of the following activities outside of class. Bring the information you find out back to class.

1. Take the questions that you and your partner prepared in the preceding class activity. Go to or call one of the places or people you listed to find out the answers to your questions. Write a report on a separate piece of paper or make an oral presentation to the class that summarizes the information you found out.

   Notes

2. Either individually or with a partner, think of a place or person that you need to get information from, such as

   - a car rental or car insurance agency,
   - an apartment rental agency,
   - an appliance store,
   - the telephone company,
   - a potential employer,
   - a sports club, or
   - a private writing tutor.

   Write questions that you think will help you get the information you need. Then ask an American native speaker of English what questions he/she would ask in the same situation. Are your questions similar to or somewhat different from the American's question?

Your questions   American's questions

Combine your questions and then call or go to the place where you can best find out the answers to your questions. (Ask the American where he/she would go if you don't know.) Take notes. Then, write a summary of the information on a separate piece of paper, or present it to the class.

Notes

Class Activity (work in pairs)

You are interested in applying for a two-year scholarship in your field of study at a North American university. Decide what information you would ask the official in charge of selecting applicants. Then, together with your partner, formulate questions that you would ask. Present your questions to the class for discussion.

Part Two: Using Questions to Carry on a Conversation

 Warm-up

1. What if you met a friend after summer vacation and asked, "Did you have a nice summer vacation?" What purpose does this question serve? Is it only to get information? If you're interested in continuing the conversation on this topic, how would you indicate this to your friend?

2. What are some ways you can show a person you are interested in carrying on a conversation?

3. How do you feel when you're in a conversation and you ask all the questions?

4. Why might you hesitate to ask someone questions?

Dialogues for Analysis

Conversation between Beth and Jose

Situation: Jose is sitting at the pool of his apartment complex. His neighbor, Beth, comes and sits down next to him.

Dialogue 1

Beth:	Hi, Jose.
Jose:	Hi.
Beth:	My roommate told me you just got a job with a television station.
Jose:	Yes, I did.
Beth:	That's great! What station is it?
Jose:	BCD in New York.
Beth:	When do you start?
Jose:	Next month.
Beth:	Are you looking forward to living in New York?
Jose:	Yes.
Beth:	Well, I hope you enjoy your new job.
Jose:	Thanks.

Two-sided Conversation

Dialogue 2

Beth:	Hi, Jose.
Jose:	Hi, Beth. How's it going?
Beth:	Fine. Hey, my roommate told me you just got a job with a television station.
Jose:	Yeah, in New York City at Station BCD. I start next month.
Beth:	Are you looking forward to living in New York?
Jose:	I think so. It seems like an exciting place, but I've only been there once. Have you ever been there?
Beth:	I used to live there.
Jose:	You did? That's great! Maybe you can tell me where I should look for an apartment.
Beth:	Sure. Why don't you stop by this evening, and I can give you some information.
Jose:	Thanks. I'd really appreciate that.
Beth:	OK. See you this evening.

Dialogue Analysis

1. In both dialogues, how does Beth begin the conversation with Jose?

2. What topic does Beth choose to talk about? Why does she select this topic?

3. In either of the dialogues, does Jose ask Beth questions? What might this show?

4. What's the difference in the way Jose answers Beth in dialogues 1 and 2?

5. How would you feel if you were Beth in dialogue 1?

6. What would you do if you were Beth in dialogue 1?

7. If you're interested in carrying on a conversation with someone, what are some things you can do to show you are interested?

8. If you're not interested in carrying on a conversation with someone, what are some things you can do to show you are disinterested?

▶ Points to Remember

1. In English, questions can be used to get specific information. They are also used to carry on a conversation.
2. Sometimes a simple question can keep the conversation going and/or indicate an interest in continuing it.
3. Both speakers should be prepared to ask each other questions. If one speaker has to ask all the questions, he/she may feel the other speaker is not interested in a conversation.
4. Short answers to questions sometimes are perceived as an unwillingness on the part of the speaker to share information or a desire to end the conversation.

Class Activity (work in pairs)

Your teacher will team you with another student. On a separate sheet of paper, together rewrite the following dialogue between Alex and Elena. Make changes that show more willingness on Elena's part to carry on a conversation with Alex. Share your dialogue with other class members. Or, your instructor may collect the dialogues and give you feedback and/or choose a few dialogues to read to the class.

One-sided Conversation

Situation: Alex and Elena have arranged to meet for coffee after work.

Alex: Hi, Elena.
Elena: Hi.
Alex: Did you have a good day today?
Elena: Pretty good.
Alex: Anything special happen?
Elena: Nothing much.
Alex: What are you going to do this weekend?
Elena: I don't know yet.
Alex: There's a good movie in town that I saw last night.
Elena: Oh.

Community Activity

Choose from the following activities to do outside of class. Share your observations with the class.

1. Ask an American what questions he/she would ask in one or two of the following situations. Write down the questions and bring them to class for discussion.
   a. A friend of yours belongs to a singles group that has many social activities for unmarried people. You want to find out about it and what its members do.

b. Your friend has a new baby daughter. You're interested in finding out about the baby and how she has changed your friend's life.

c. You heard that a friend of yours plays a musical instrument. You want to find out more about the friend's interest in music and perhaps discuss the possibility of playing together sometime.

2. Begin a conversation with an American acquaintance. Ask the American a few questions to keep the conversation going. Write down the topics you discussed and the questions you asked. Did the American seem interested or uninterested in carrying on a conversation with you? How could you tell? Present the topics and questions to members of the class and share your observations about the conversation.

Notes

Final Activity (role-play in pairs)

Your teacher will group you with another student and assign you one of the following role-plays for you to prepare. First, discuss the role-play and decide what questions might help the conversation work. Be prepared to perform the role-play in front of the class. The teacher and the other students will discuss each role-play presented and make comments on how it can be improved.

1. You're at a party and you see a friend who has been studying English at a well-known institute. You are thinking about studying English there. This seems like a good topic to talk about.
2. You find out that a friend of yours has been accepted at an American university. You are happy for him/her and want to get more details.
3. You see a friend who has just joined a club or sports team. You really like sports and are interested in finding out more about the club or team.
4. Your friend has a new job. You're interested in finding out how she's/he's getting along.
5. A friend introduces you to a foreign visitor on vacation in your town. You're interested in finding out what the visitor has seen and done on his/her trip and what his/her impressions are.

Notes

3
Using the Telephone

 Warm-up

1. How often do you usually use the telephone each day?

2. What are some of the reasons you use the phone?

3. Do you ever need to speak English on the telephone? When?

4. Is it easier to speak English on the phone or face-to-face? Why or why not? What problems have you had using English on the phone? What do you think has caused the problems?

Dialogues for Analysis

Invitation by Telephone

Dialogue 1

> *Mary:* Hello.
> *Barb:* Hi, Mary. It's Barb.
> *Mary:* Oh, hi! How's it going?
> *Barb:* Fine. Jack, Mike, and I are going to the football game on Saturday. We've got an extra ticket. Do you want to go with us?
> *Mary:* Sure. I'd love to go.
> *Barb:* Great. It starts at one so we can stop by for you about 12:30.
> *Mary:* That's fine. I'll be ready.
> *Barb:* OK, so we'll see you Saturday.
> *Mary:* OK, see you then. Thanks a lot.

Dialogue 2

> *Mary:* Hello.
> *Anne:* Hi, Mary. This is Anne Ashley. I met you in chem class the other day.
> *Mary:* Oh, hi Anne. How are you?
> *Anne:* Fine. How do you like the class?
> *Mary:* It's a lot of work but I like the professor.
> *Anne:* Me too. Hey, my roommate and I are going to the ballroom dancing classes Saturday night in the Student Union. I remember you said you liked to dance, so I was thinking you might want to go with us.
> *Mary:* Sure. That sounds great. I've been wanting to go to those.
> *Anne:* Good. How about if we meet you outside the Union at 8:00.
> *Mary:* That's fine.
> *Anne:* OK. Then, we'll see you Saturday.
> *Mary:* OK. Thanks a lot. Bye-bye.
> *Anne:* Bye.

Dialogue Analysis

1. What is the purpose of these calls?

2. In both dialogues, who speaks first, the caller or the answerer?

3. How is Barb's opening in dialogue 1 different from Anne's in dialogue 2? Why do you think they are different?

4. Which dialogue has more small talk? What do you think the purpose of the small talk is?

5. In the two dialogues, who ends each conversation, and how is it done? What is the purpose of saying "so" and "then" before "we'll see you Saturday"?

6. In both dialogues, what is the purpose of the "OKs" toward the end of the call?

 # Dialogue for Analysis

Calling the Doctor

Receptionist: Good afternoon, Family Physicians. May I help you?

Patient: Yes, thank you. This is Jim Johnson. I'm a patient of Dr. Martin's, and I'd like to make an appointment for a checkup.

Receptionist: The doctor has a really busy schedule right now. If it's not urgent, there's a month wait for an appointment.

Patient: Oh, that's fine. I'm not in any hurry. Is anything available on the fifteenth of next month?

Receptionist: Let's see. Yes, the fifteenth at 9:00 a.m. is open.

Patient: That'll be fine.

Receptionist: All right. See you on the fifteenth, Mr. Johnson.

Patient: OK. Thanks a lot. Bye.

Receptionist: Good-bye.

Dialogue Analysis

1. How does the receptionist answer the phone differently than Mary in dialogues 1 and 2?

2. How does the caller introduce himself in this dialogue? Why?

3. Why doesn't the receptionist introduce herself?

4. What is the purpose of this call? Does the caller clearly state the purpose?

5. Is there any small talk?

6. How do the receptionist and the patient signal that the conversation is finished?

Short Dialogues for Analysis: Expressions Used on the Telephone

Wrong Number*

Dialogue 1 (telephone rings)

A: Hello.
C: Hello. Is this Bob?
A: I'm sorry. You have the wrong number.
C: Oh, I'm sorry.

Dialogue 2 (telephone rings)

A: Hello.
C: May I speak to Mrs. Brant please?
A: I'm afraid you have the wrong number.
C: Is this 555–1140?
A: No, it isn't.
C: Oh, I'm sorry.

Wrong Number Dialogue Analysis

1. In dialogues 1 and 2, how does A tell C he has the wrong number?

2. In dialogue 2, how does C verify that she has the wrong number? Why doesn't C ask A what his/her telephone number is?

Answering the Phone for Someone Else

Dialogue 1 (telephone rings)

A: Hello.
C: Hello. May I speak to Kathy Burns please?
A: Just a minute, please. (Turns from the telephone.) Kathy, telephone.

Dialogue 2 (telephone rings)

A: Hello.
C: Hello. Is Larry home?
A: I'm sorry. He isn't here right now. May I take a message?

---

*note that A = Answerer and C = Caller whenever these initials are used in a telephone conversation.

Answering the Phone for Someone Else Dialogue Analysis

1. In dialogue 1, how does the answerer indicate that she is not Kathy, but that Kathy is home?

2. In dialogue 2, what does the answerer say when the caller asks for Larry?

3. Does either answerer ask the caller to identify himself/herself?

Formal vs. Intimate
Dialogue 1 (telephone rings)

A: Hello.
C: Hello. Is this Dr. Waring's residence?
A: Yes. This is Dr. Waring speaking.
C: Dr. Waring, this is Norman Grant from the *Hamilton News*.

Dialogue 2 (telephone rings)

A: Hello.
C: Hi. What are you doing?
A: Just reading the paper. When are you coming home?
C: I just called to say I'm on my way.
A: OK. See you soon.
C: Bye.

Formal vs. Intimate Dialogue Analysis

1. In which dialogue do you think the caller and the answerer know each other well? How can you tell this?

2. Is dialogue 1 a business or a social call? How do you know this?

3. In dialogue 2, what do you think the relationship between the caller and the answerer is?

Answering Machine

A: Hello. We can't come to the phone right now. Please leave a message and we will get back to you as soon as possible.
C: Hi, Liz. This is Sam Osborn. Can you give me a call if you still want to borrow my tent? I'm at 555–0315.

Answering Machine Dialogue Analysis

1. What does the caller include in his message to Liz?

2. What if Sam doesn't hear from Liz? Will he call her back?

3. Why doesn't the answering machine say "No one is home right now"?

Class Activity (pair or small group work)

Appropriate vs. Inappropriate or Incorrect Dialogues

Your instructor will place you in pairs or small groups and assign you the following task. Rewrite the examples in bold-face type in the left column to make them more appropriate or correct. Use the previous dialogues as examples if you are uncertain about what is wrong. Discuss your changes with the class.

Inappropriate	Appropriate

Dialogue 1 (example)

A: Hello.
C: Hello. Is Marty there?
A: **Who is this?**   This is Marty. *or* Just a moment, please. *or* Yes, he is. May I say who's calling?

Dialogue 2

A: Hello.
C: Hello. Could I talk to Kim please?
A: **Please wait a minute.**

Dialogue 3

A: Hello.
C: Hello. Is Nancy Turner home?
A: **Wrong number** (A hangs up).

Dialogue 4

A: Hello.
C: Hello. Is Rex there?
A: **He's not here. Good-bye.**

Dialogue 5

A: English Language Center.
C: Hello. **I want to talk to Dr. Smith.**

Dialogue 6

A: Hello.
C: Hello, Hank. **I'm Mohammed.**

A: Oh, hi, Mohammed.

Dialogue 7

A: Hello.
C: **Is Irma here?**

Dialogue 8

A: Hello. Dr. Casey's office.
C: Hello. **May I speak to her?**

Dialogue 9

A: Hello.
C: Hello. May I speak to Janet?
A: She's not here right now. **May I leave a message?**

Dialogue 10

A: Hello.
C: Hello. Is Mr. Allen Mason home?
A: I'm sorry, **but he isn't here.** (meaning wrong number)

Points to Remember

1. There are conventional expressions that we use on the telephone such as "Just a minute, please." "This is Marsha . . . Can (may) I take a message?" And "I'm sorry, you have the wrong number." If we modify these expressions, they may sound strange or inappropriate, as in "Wait a minute, please." or "I am Marsha."

2. We introduce ourselves casually to friends on the telephone (e.g., "Hi, this is Sam." Or "Hi, it's Nicole."). However, if we call someone we do not know or who we think won't recognize our voice, we usually introduce ourselves more formally (e.g., by stating our relationship to the person, as in "Hello, this is Sam Osborn, your neighbor.").

3. Business calls may differ from personal calls. For example, in a business call, the caller may be asked to identify him-/herself to the receptionist or person who answers the phone. In a personal call, it may depend on the situation, such as the caller's relationship with the person who answers the phone.

4. When we want to close a telephone conversation we begin to wind the conversation down by using expressions such as "so," "then," "well," "well then," or "OK."

5. Answering machines are commonly used today. The answering machine gives the caller instructions. If the caller wishes to leave a message, he/she waits for the beep (or series of beeps) and then generally says his/her name, phone number, and a short message with instructions for the person.

Homework and Community Activity

For homework, answer the following questions. Your teacher may assign you specific questions to answer. To get this information, you may need to use a local telephone book or directory and/or ask an American. The class will discuss the information you have gathered the next day in class.

1. In case of an emergency, what number should you dial?

2. What numbers would you call to find out information about the following:
   a. time

   b. weather (if available)

   c. international calls

3. If you want to find out your neighbor's telephone number and don't have a telephone directory, how would you locate the number?

4. What is your area code?

5. How can you find out the area code for Phoenix, Arizona?

6. How do you find out the telephone number of someone who is not living in your own city?

7. In order to make a call to your home country from the United States, what numbers would you have to dial before you dial your home telephone number?

8. What does it mean to make a direct-dial long distance call? How is this done?

9. What does it mean to call someone person-to-person? To call person-to-person, you need to make an operator assisted call. How would you do this?

10. What does calling someone collect mean? How do you do this?

11. Are long-distance calls always the same price, no matter the long-distance service, the day of the week, or the time of day?

12. How much does it cost to make a local call from a pay phone?

13. What is a calling card? How does it work?

14. How do you get a telephone installed in your home? Explain some of the options available, such as touch-tone, call waiting, and call forwarding? Do these options generally cost extra?

 Final Activity (role-play in pairs or groups of threes)

Your teacher will group you with two other students and assign one of the following role-plays for you to prepare. First, discuss the role-play with the rest of your group, then practice what you would say in this situation. Be prepared to perform the role-play in front of the class. The teacher and the other students will discuss and compare each role-play presented and make comments on how it can be improved.

1. You are trying to call your friend. You dial the wrong number by mistake. You call again and your friend answers the phone. You want to borrow something from him/her. Make arrangements to get it. Then conclude the conversation.

2. You call the office of your advisor, Dr. Black, in order to make an appointment. Dr. Black isn't in his/her office. The secretary asks you to call back later that afternoon. You call again and the secretary puts the call through to Dr. Black. You ask for an appointment to talk about courses you would like to take next semester. Arrange a time that you can meet. Then conclude the conversation.

3. You would like private conversation classes in English (or another language). Call a friend who gives you the name and telephone number of a native speaker who offers classes. Then call the native speaker and find out if he/she gives conversation classes, how much they cost, and if it's possible to arrange evening classes. Then conclude the conversation.

4. You call a friend for help with something. One of your friend's parents answers the telephone. Your friend isn't home, but you leave a message to have him/her call you. Your friend calls you back.

Notes

4

Invitations

 Warm-up

1. Have you received any invitations recently? Where were you invited to? What were the circumstances?

2. If you're offering someone an invitation, what information does the person need to know before deciding to accept the invitation or to turn it down?

3. If you ask someone out to dinner or to the movies in your country, does it automatically mean that you will pay the entire check? What determines who pays?

Dialogues for Analysis

Dialogue 1

Rich: My wife and I were wondering if you would like to come to dinner on Sunday.

Gino: Sure. That sounds really nice.

Rich: Good. How about around 5:00?

Gino: That's fine. What can I bring?

Rich: Just yourself.

Gino: OK. Thanks a lot. Oh, what's your address?

Rich: It's 240 Lincoln, right across from the public tennis courts.

Gino: I know where that is. OK. Thanks a lot for the invitation and I'll see you Sunday.

Dialogue Analysis

1. From the dialogue, what can you tell about the relationship between Rich and Gino?

2. What expression does Rich use to invite Gino? What does Gino say to accept?

3. What information does Rich give Gino when he makes the invitation? What about after Gino accepts?

4. After Gino accepts the invitation to dinner, he asks if he can bring something. Is this customary? What might Rich have asked Gino to bring? Do you think Gino will bring something anyway?

Dialogue 2

Katie: Hey, Karen.

Karen: Hi, Katie.

Katie: Did you pass your driver's test?

Karen: Yes, and no mistakes, either.

Katie: Congratulations! Do you have time for a cup of coffee to celebrate?

Karen: Sure.

Katie: How about going to Carlo's or Saxon's?

Karen: Let's go to Saxon's. We haven't been there in a long time.

Katie: OK. Good.

Dialogue Analysis

1. Why does Katie say she is inviting Karen to coffee? Do you think this is the only reason? How does she offer (make) the invitation?

2. How do Katie and Karen decide which place they are going to go?

3. What is the relationship between Karen and Katie? How can you tell? Do you think they see each other often?

4. Who do you think will pay for the coffee? Who do you think usually pays?

Dialogue 3

Dana: Hello?
Gary: Hello, Dana?
Dana: Yes?
Gary: This is Gary Kingsley from Ski Club.
Dana: Oh, hi. How are you?
Gary: Fine. I just called to see if you'd like to go to the movies tonight.
Dana: Oh, I'm sorry, I can't. I have to work tonight.
Gary: How about Saturday?
Dana: I'm going away for the weekend, but thanks anyway for the invitation.
Gary: OK. I'll give you a call some other time.

Dialogue Analysis

1. What is the relationship between Dana and Gary? Do you think they are boyfriend and girlfriend? Good friends? Acquaintances? How can you tell?

2. How many times does Gary invite Dana to the movies? How does Dana reject Gary's invitations? What excuses does she give? Is she polite?

3. Does Dana want to go out with Gary? How can you tell?

4. After Gary says "OK. I'll give you a call some other time," what might Dana say if she wanted Gary to call her back? What do you think she probably said?

5. How can you let a person know that you would like to go out with him/her?

6. Do you think Gary will call back?

7. What are some ways you can let a person know you aren't interested in going out with him/her?

Dialogue 4

Carol: How about lunch?
Bob: Sure. I'm just finishing up these reports.
Carol: No rush. Stop by my office when you're ready.

Dialogue Analysis

1. How does Carol extend the invitation to lunch?

2. How do Bob and Carol know each other? Do you think they eat lunch together a lot?

3. Will one person pay for lunch, or will Bob and Carol split the check?

Invitation Expressions

Offers

Informal	General
1. How about coming to . . . ?	1. I was wondering if you'd like to go to . . . .
2. Do you have time to go to . . . ?	2. Would you like to go to . . . ?
3. Let's go to	3. I'd like to invite you to . . . .
4. How'd you like to . . . ?	
5. Do you want to (wanna) go to . . . ?	

Acceptances

Informal	General
1. Sure.	1. Thanks. That sounds like fun. (That sounds nice.)
2. OK.	2. Thank you. That's very nice of you.

Rejections

Informal	General
1. I can't. I've gotta . . .	1. I'd really like to, but I have to . . . . Thanks for the invitation, though.
	2. I wish I could, but I have to . . . . Thanks, anyway.
	3. I'm sorry. I'm not going to be able to make it because I have to . . . . But thanks for the invitation.

Note: Sometimes the person who receives the invitation cannot immediately accept or reject it. If it doesn't inconvenience the person offering the invitation, it may be possible to give a tentative answer such as:

- Thanks. I'll check with my wife. Can I let you know tomorrow?
- I'm not sure if I can make it because some friends of mine may be coming from out of town.

▶ Points to Remember

1. When you extend an invitation, it is important to include the time and place and other useful information.
2. After the invitation is accepted, the two people may need to discuss other things such as a meeting place (the address and directions on how to get there), the exact time, transportation, other guests, suitable clothing, what to bring, etc.
3. Whether you accept or reject an invitation, it is usually customary to show pleasure at receiving the invitation and to thank the person who invited you.

4. It is usually considered polite to offer an excuse when rejecting an invitation. However, the excuse can be rather vague or even avoided. (*Examples:* "I'm busy Sunday, but it was nice of you to invite me." Or "I can't make it Friday. Maybe we can get together another time.")

5. There is often no clear-cut answer to the question of who pays. However, if a person extends a formal invitation, he/she will generally be expected to or want to pay. Also, if the purpose of the invitation is to celebrate a birthday, graduation, or another event, the guest of honor is generally not expected to pay. However, if two friends or work associates routinely get together for coffee or lunch, or an evening out, it is generally the case that each will pay their own bill unless they have a different agreement.

Class Activity (work in pairs or groups of threes)

Your teacher will group you with one or two other students. Together read the following dialogues. Suggest ways the bold-face part in each dialogue can be changed or expanded to make the dialogue more appropriate. Write down your suggestions. All of the characters in the dialogues are acquaintances.

Leslie: Hi, Ahmed. I'm going to lunch. Do you wanna go?
Ahmed: **I can't go.**

Tom: I'm having a party Saturday. **Would you mind coming?**
Ana: Sounds like fun.

Cindy: Would you like to go shopping tomorrow?
Carla: **I don't know.**

Jessie: Would you like to go to the movies tonight?
Andrea: **I have to wash my hair.**

Kim: Do you want to go to a football game with me Saturday?
John: **No, I don't like football.**

Class Activity (work in pairs)

Your teacher will team you with another student and assign you the following task:

> You would like to invite your partner somewhere. Decide together an appropriate place to go. The invitation can be formal or informal. Then practice giving the invitation. Be sure to include the necessary information. Your partner can either accept or reject the invitation. If he/she rejects the invitation, he/she should offer an excuse. If he/she accepts, the two of you may need to discuss more details, depending on the type of invitation. Present your invitation to the class. Compare differences among the invitations presented and talk about what they might be attributed to. Also discuss how the invitations can be improved.

Homework Activity

The teacher will assign you one of the following two role-plays to write on a separate paper. One of the role-plays is formal, and the other is informal. Be prepared to share your role-play with the class and discuss how and why the first role-play should differ from the second.

1. You invite your boss to dinner. Specify the time, day, and place. Your boss accepts the invitation. Together discuss the details.

2. You invite a good friend to dinner. Specify the time, day and place. Your friend accepts the invitation. Together discuss the details.

Community Activity

Do the following two activities outside of class. First, interview an American about invitation customs in the United States. Then interview someone from your own country. Make cultural comparisons. Be prepared to discuss at least three of your findings in a short, informal speech.

1. Interview an American and take notes on his or her response to at least four of the following questions.

    a. If you were invited to a friend's house for dinner, would you bring anything, such as a gift, food, etc.?

    b. If you were invited to a party by a coworker and her husband, what would you wear?

    c. If someone invited you to dinner at 7:00, what time would you plan to arrive? If someone invited you to an informal party at 8:00, what time would you plan to arrive?

    d. If you accepted an invitation to a friend's house and you remembered later that you had already received another invitation, what would you do?

    e. If you and a good friend went out for coffee, who would pay? Would it make any difference if it were a man or a woman? If a man asks a woman to the movies, who do you think should pay?

f. Do you think it is proper for a woman to invite a man on a date?

g. If a friend invited you to a party and you couldn't go unless you got a ride, what would you say?

2. Interview a friend from your own country. Ask your friend the same questions that you asked the American concerning invitation customs. Take notes, make cultural comparisons, and then prepare your presentation in which you list similarities and differences you found.

Notes

 Final Activity (small group discussion)

Your teacher will group you with two other students. Take turns presenting the findings from your oral interviews to your group in the form of a short speech. Discuss cultural differences. Or, your instructor may ask you to give your speech to the class as a whole.

5

"Excuse Me" and "I'm Sorry"

 Warm-up

1. What are some ways of getting a person's attention?

2. In your country, if you wanted to get a waiter's attention, how would you do it?

3. How would you get a waiter's attention in the United States?

4. If you wanted to get your instructor's attention during class, how would you do it in your country?

Dialogues for Analysis A

Dialogue 1

Situation: A man and a woman are sitting in the dentist's office. After a while, the woman turns to the man and asks for the time.

Woman: Excuse me, do you know what time it is?
Man: Let's see. It's exactly 2 o'clock.

Question: Why does the woman say "Excuse me" to the man?

Dialogue 2

Situation: Ben is having some friends over for dinner. They have just sat down to eat.

Karen: Ben, this soup is delicious. (The telephone rings.)
Ben: Excuse me. I'll be right back.

Question: Why does Ben say "Excuse me"?

Dialogue 3

Situation: A woman is on a crowded bus and she needs to get off at the next stop. There is a man standing between her and the door.

Woman (to man):   Excuse me.

Question: Why does the woman say "Excuse me" to the man?

Dialogue 4

Situation: Frank and Joanne work together in a shoe store. Frank is helping a shopper try on a pair of shoes. Joanne comes to ask Frank a question.

Frank (to shopper):   We have that shoe in white and yellow.
Joanne: Excuse me, Frank. Do you know the price of these brown sandals?
Frank: They're $26.

Question: Why does Joanne say "Excuse me" to Frank?

Dialogue Analysis

1. In dialogue 1, the woman gets the man's attention by saying "Excuse me." If she knew the man, would she still say "Excuse me"?

2. Is "Excuse me" used for the same purpose in dialogues 1 and 2?

3. In dialogue 3, why do you think the woman feels that she has to say something?

4. Joanne uses "Excuse me" in dialogue 4. Could she have said, "Hey Frank"? When is "Hey" appropriate?

▶ Points to Remember

1. We commonly use the expression "Excuse me" in English when we *(a)* try to get someone's attention; *(b)* leave a conversation before it is finished; *(c)* ask someone to move or when walking in front of someone; or *(d)* interrupt someone.
2. "Excuse me" is commonly used in formal situations or when the speakers do not know each other well. However, it is sometimes too formal to use with friends.
3. "Hey" is used with friends in informal situations to get someone's attention.

Dialogues for Analysis B

Dialogue 1

Situation: After class, Youssef goes to tell something to his instructor, Paul.

Youssef: Excuse me, Paul.
Paul: Yes?
Youssef: I'm sorry I didn't do my homework yesterday. Can I give it to you tomorrow?
Paul: OK.

Question: Why does Youssef say "I'm sorry" to Paul?

Dialogue 2

Situation: Linda is at a party. She accidentally hits a glass of wine with her arm and some of it spills on the floor. The hostess, Nancy, comes to help her clean it up.

Linda: I'm really sorry, Nancy.
Nancy: Don't worry about it. Here, let me help you clean it up.

Question: Why does Linda say "I'm sorry" to Nancy?

Dialogue 3

Situation: Paula and her older sister Penny are having an argument.

Paula: Would you please stop criticizing my clothes. I don't tell you what to wear.
Penny: You're right. I'm sorry.

Question: Why does Penny say "I'm sorry" to Paula?

Dialogue Analysis

1. In dialogue 1, why does Youssef feel the need to say "I'm sorry"? What was his responsibility? Why wouldn't "Excuse me" be appropriate in this case?

2. In dialogue 2, how does Linda emphasize that she is sorry? Why do you think she says "I'm sorry" instead of "Excuse me"?

3. In dialogue 3, what does Paula think Penny has done wrong? How does Penny show that she knows she's at fault?

▶ ## Points to Remember

1. We usually use "I'm sorry" when we think we have hurt or offended someone; for example, when we forget something, when we are late, when we spill a drink, when we recognize we have insulted someone, or when we may have hurt someone physically or emotionally.

2. "I'm sorry" tends to show a sincere concern for a person's feelings.

Dialogues for Analysis C

Dialogue 1

Situation: Fred is having a Homeless Shelter meeting at his house this week. His friend, Laura, comes without her husband, Jim.

> *Fred:*   Hi, Laura. Where's Jim?
> *Laura:*   He had to go to Chicago because his mother is in the hospital.
> *Fred:*   Oh, I'm sorry. Is it anything serious?

Question: Why does Fred say "I'm sorry" to Laura?

Dialogue 2

Situation: Omar wants to buy a drink from the vending machine, but he only has a dollar. He sees his friend, Gina.

> *Omar:*   Gina, do you have change for a dollar?
> *Gina:*   I'm sorry. All I have is a quarter.

Question: Why does Gina say "I'm sorry" to Omar?

Dialogue 3

Situation: A woman brings her dog into a supermarket.

> *Woman:*   Can I bring my dog in here?
> *Clerk:*   I'm sorry, but pets aren't permitted in the store. It's a state law.

Question: Why does the clerk say "I'm sorry"?

Dialogue Analysis

1. In dialogue 1, did Fred say "I'm sorry" because he had hurt or offended someone?

2. In dialogue 2, was it Gina's responsibility to have change for her friend? If not, why was it necessary to say "I'm sorry"?

3. In dialogue 3, why does the clerk say, "It's a state law"?

► Points to Remember

In addition to using "I'm sorry" when we may have hurt or offended someone, we also use "I'm sorry" to express regret or sympathy for another person or a situation in general; for example,

(1) when someone is seriously ill and dies;
(2) when we can't help someone who has requested help;
(3) when an unfortunate situation can't be changed;
(4) when you have to tell someone bad news; or
(5) when you are not able to accept an invitation.

Class Activity (to be done by the class as a whole)

Look at the examples of "Excuse me" and "I'm sorry" (boldfaced) in the following dialogue. Tell how each is used.

Situation: Mary needs to talk to her advisor, Dr. Clark, about what classes she should take next semester. She goes to her office to talk to her.

Mary:	**Excuse me,** Dr. Clark.
Dr. Clark:	Come in, Mary.
Mary:	Do you have time to talk to me now about registration for next semester?
Dr. Clark:	**I'm sorry,** I have a class right now, but I could see you at 3:30 or 4:00.
Mary:	Four o'clock is fine. I'll come back then.
(At 4:15)	
Mary:	**I'm sorry** I'm late, Dr. Clark. My bus was late.
Dr. Clark:	That's all right. Come in and sit down. **Excuse me** for a minute while I get your folder from the secretary.

Community Activity

For homework ask an American whether he/she would use "Excuse me" or "I'm sorry" in the following situations. If the American wouldn't use these forms, what would he/she say? Write down the American's answers and be prepared to present them to the class.

1. You come late to class. The professor has already started the lesson.

2. You cause a car accident. You go to talk to the other driver.

3. You go to a concert and want to get to your seat, but a person is blocking the aisle.

4. You're in class but don't feel well. You decide that you have no choice but to leave early even though the professor is in the middle of the lecture.

5. You are walking down the street; you see a good friend ahead of you and want her to wait for you.

6. You're at a party and want to go to the bathroom, but don't know where it is so you ask another guest.

7. You're having a party and there is a group of three people smoking inside your house. Smoke bothers you a lot, and you want people to go outside to the porch to smoke.

8. You're having pizza with some friends you invited to your house, and the doorbell rings.

9. A friend has just found out he lost his job.

10. The grandmother of a friend of yours just died. You see the friend on the street.

Homework Activity

Read the following situations. Then, on a separate sheet of paper, write a short conversation for each situation in which the speakers use "Excuse me" or "I'm sorry." Share your conversations with the class.

1. Rob is looking for the First National Bank. He stops a stranger on the street and asks for directions. The stranger, who is a foreigner, tells Ben that he doesn't know where it is either.
   Example:

   Rob: Excuse me, could you tell me where the First National Bank is?

   Stranger:

2. David has just learned that his son has been involved in a car accident. David goes to tell his boss, Mr. Gonzalez, that he must leave work and go to the hospital. His boss is talking so David must interrupt him. Mr. Gonzalez shows sympathy for David's situation.
3. Yukiko, a foreign student, goes up to her English instructor, Alice Green and invites her to a class party at her house on Saturday. Alice would like to go, but she has to go out of town to visit family.

Final Activity (role-play in pairs)

Your teacher will group you with one other student and assign one or more of the following role-plays for you to prepare. First discuss the role-play with your partner, then practice what you would say in this situation. Use "Excuse me" and "I'm sorry" appropriately. Be prepared to perform the role-play in front of the class. The teacher and the other students will discuss and compare each role-play presented and make comments on how it can be improved.

1. Chuck is in a large supermarket. He approaches a salesperson to ask where he can find film for his camera. The salesperson politely explains that they don't sell film but that he might be able to find some film in the drugstore next door.

2. It is one o'clock in the morning. Caroline is up late listening to music in her apartment. Her neighbor comes to the door to ask her to turn down her stereo because of the noise. Caroline, who didn't realize that the music was bothering anybody, says that she will.

3. Ron is walking toward the coffee shop. He accidentally hits the arm of a young woman who walks past him. Her books spill all over the ground, and Ron begins to help her pick them up. Suddenly he recognizes her. She is a friend of his from high school named Nancy, whom he hasn't seen in years. He talks to her for a minute, and then invites her to join him for a cup of coffee. She can't go because she has a class.

Notes

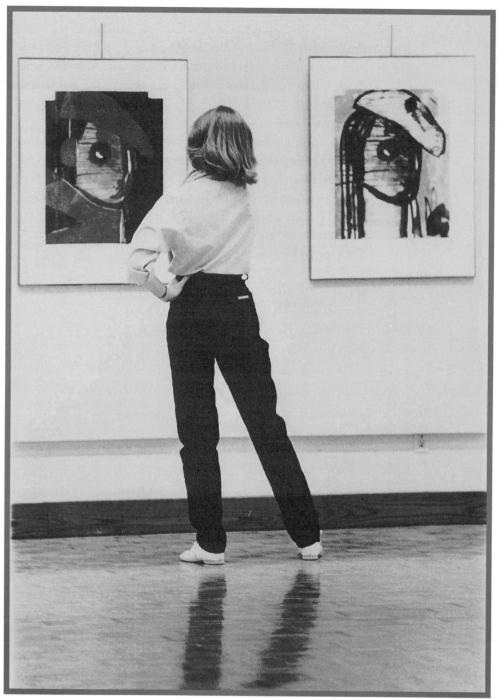

6

Making Choices—
Comparing and Contrasting

 Warm-up

1. What do you consider important in choosing an apartment?

2. If there were two apartments you liked and you had to choose one, what would be the most important factor in your decision?

3. Do you usually make decisions on your own, or do you talk about it with somebody? Who?

Dialogue for Analysis

Apartment Hunting

Situation: Dan and Bill are friends who study at the university together. They want to be roommates for the coming year and have been looking at apartments. They've found two apartments they like and now need to decide which one they'll choose.

Dan: What do you think? Which apartment do you like better?

Bill: Well, the modern one's really nice, but the older one's definitely bigger.

Dan: Yeah. In the older one we could use the dining room for a study.

Bill: Mm-hmm. But the bedrooms in the modern one are pretty spacious and the furniture is nicer.

Dan: But the older apartment's cheaper.

Bill: Well, not that much cheaper, only $30.00.

Dan: That's true. And you're right. The modern one is nicer looking. Then again, modern apartments look nice, but sometimes the walls are so thin that you can hear every word your neighbors say.

Bill: Yeah. That wouldn't be so good if we're doing a lot of studying. On the other hand, though, the kitchen in the modern apartment is really nice. The refrigerator is huge and there's a disposal and a dishwasher. It would save us a lot of time.

Dan: You seem to like the modern one more.

Bill: Um, I guess I do. But really, I could live in either one.

Dan: Yeah, me too. I guess the question is, do we want roominess or luxury?

Bill: I don't know. Maybe I am more interested in luxury.

Dan: OK. Then let's get the modern one.

Bill: You sure?

Dan: Really. I like 'em both.

Bill: OK. The modern one it is, then.

Dialogue Analysis

1. What is the purpose of this conversation?

2. What do Dan and Bill spend a lot of time doing in the conversation?

3. How can Dan tell that Bill likes the modern apartment better?

4. If Bill likes the modern apartment better, why doesn't he say so at the beginning of the conversation?

5. What about Dan? Is it clear which apartment he prefers?

6. Why does Bill say, "But really, I could live in either one"?

7. When Dan says, "Let's get the modern one," why does Bill say "You sure?"

8. What purpose do the expressions "but," "then again," and "on the other hand" serve in the dialogue?

9. If you and a friend were trying to choose between two apartments, do you think making a series of comparisons would be helpful? Why or why not?

10. Which apartment would you choose? Why?

11. If Bill and Dan had not agreed on which apartment to get, what would some alternatives be?

Points to Remember

1. Before making an important decision, Americans usually discuss the alternatives. One common way they do this is to compare and contrast aspects of each alternative in order to make a more careful decision.

2. When making an important decision with another person, a speaker may purposely choose not to state a definite preference without first making some comparisons or trying to get an idea of the other person's preference. In order to find out someone's preference, questions such as "What do you think?" "What's your impression?" or "Which one would you get?" are sometimes used.

3. Expressions such as "then again," "on the other hand," and "but" are frequently used in decision making to introduce a different or opposing point of view.

4. Comparatives and superlatives such as "bigger," "the most durable," and "less expensive," are frequently used to highlight differences. "*As* + ADJECTIVE + *as*," (as good as) and "the same" are used to point out similarities.

5. When making a choice with someone, we may use comparisons persuasively as a way of getting someone to agree or change his or her mind. We may emphasize the positive aspects of the alternative we like best and point out the negative aspects of the alternative we don't want.

Class Activity (work in pairs)

Discuss with your instructor what information you would want to know before choosing a university.

You and a friend would like to study at a university in the United States. You have both been accepted at two universities—Carlson University and Lincoln University. Now you have to decide which of the two you prefer. You will be given some information that may help you make a decision. In pairs, compare the two universities, discussing their advantages and disadvantages. Make as many comparisons as you can from the information you have. Then decide together which university you would choose. If possible, you would both like to go to the same university. Present your comparisons and final decision to the class for discussion.

Carlson University

Location: Small City, U.S.A.
Tuition: approximately $9,500 per semester, nonresidents; $3,500, residents
Type: State university with a graduate school
Number of Students: 35,000
Average Class Size: 20
Reputation: Good reputation in all areas, especially good in economics, business administration, computer science, law, linguistics, psychology, biological sciences, music, drama, and education.
Room and Board: Dormitories with cafeteria are generally available for undergraduate students only. The cost per person for a double room is about $3,400 per semester, including all meals, except Sunday dinner. Most graduate students live off campus in apartments. The cost of a one-bedroom apartment near campus generally ranges from $500–$700.

Lincoln University

Location: Big City, U.S.A.
Tuition: $10,200 per semester
Type: Private university with a graduate school
Number of Students: 10,000
Average Class Size: 17
Reputation: Good reputation in all areas, particularly in engineering, dentistry, medicine, public health, architecture, economics, physical sciences, and natural resources.
Room and Board: Both undergraduate and graduate dormitories with cafeteria available. The cost per person for a double room is $3,450 per semester, including all meals except Sunday dinner. Off-campus housing is also available, but it is rather expensive. A one-bedroom apartment generally ranges from $550–$800.
Married Student Housing: None is available. Married students should plan to live in apartments.

Married Student Housing: $425–750 per month (depending on the number of bedrooms)

Description of City: Small City, U.S.A., a town of approximately 100,000, is located in the midwestern section of the United States, about one and a half hours from a major city. The university is a 10-minute walk from Small City's downtown.

Description of City: Big City, U.S.A. is located in the eastern section of the United States. The town has a population of over 3,000,000. The university is several miles from the downtown area. Buses are available to all points in the city, and there is also a subway system that connects the city with the suburbs. There is also frequent train and bus transportation from Big City to other major East Coast cities.

Notes

Homework Activity

You are interested in buying a car. You can't afford a new car but have found four used cars to choose from. You decide to get an opinion from another member of your family or a friend. Write this person a letter comparing the cars and asking for advice. You may wish to focus on the two car(s) you like best. Include only the facts that are important to you. Here is the information that you have about the cars. Be prepared to tell the class which car you think you would choose and why.

Make and model: Toyota Corolla (LE),
    4-door sedan
Year: 1995
Asking price: $9,700
Miles: 51,000
Air bags: dual (both driver and passenger
    side)
Approximate miles per gallon: 30
Transmission: 4-speed automatic
Air conditioning: yes
Additional features: power steering,
    cruise control, power windows and
    door locks, 4-speaker stereo cassette
    and AM/FM radio
Other: in very good condition; some small
    dents on the right side; needs new
    front tires; Corollas have a reputation
    for reliability

Make and model: Volkswagen Golf III,
    four-door hatchback
Year: 1995
Asking price: $7,950
Miles: 47,000
Air bags: dual (driver and passenger)
Approximate miles per gallon: 30
Transmission: 5-speed manual
Air conditioning: no
Additional features: power steering,
    stereo AM/FM radio, sunroof
Other: clean, good condition, needs new
    brakes; a little rust near one of the
    rear tires

Make and model: Mercury Tracer LTS,
    4-door sedan
Year: 1994
Asking price: $5,300
Miles: 66,000
Air bags: single (driver side only)
Approximate miles per gallon: 28
Transmission: 4-speed automatic
Air conditioning: no
Additional features: AM/FM radio,
    cassette
Other: body in pretty good condition, ride
    a bit bumpy, needs a tune-up, cassette
    player is broken, Tracers have an
    average repair record

Make and model: Plymouth Neon, 4-door
    sedan
Year: 1995
Asking price: $6,900
Miles: 66,000
Air bags: dual (both driver and passenger
    sides)
Approximate miles per gallon: 31
Transmission: 3-speed automatic
Air conditioning: yes
Additional features: AM/FM radio, CD
    player; no cruise control
Other: somewhat noisy, scratches on
    bumper, needs a new muffler, other-
    wise, in good condition

Dear _____,

I'm faxing you this letter hoping that you can answer me as soon as possible. I've finally decided to buy a used car and I've found four cars I like, a Toyota Corolla LE, a Volkswagen Golf III, a Mercury Tracer LTS, and a Plymouth Neon. I have to make up my mind quickly and would appreciate your opinion, since you know more about cars than I do. I'm going to be studying in the United States for about three more years and need a car to get to class, shop, and take some trips during school vacation.

Thanks a lot,

_____

Community Activity

Do one of the following activities outside of class. Make comparisons, take notes, and share your information with the class. Your instructor may ask you to write the information on a separate piece of paper.

1. Compare two American newspapers. Decide which paper you would buy on a daily basis and explain why.
2. Go to the public library and look at a consumer's guide. Look up a product that you are thinking about buying, such as a television, a computer, a camera, an iron, or a car radio. Which brand and model does *Consumer's Report* recommend? Why?
3. Look at catalogues of two universities you are interested in attending. You may be able to find the catalogues in the library. Compare the universities in the same way you did in the Class Activity on page 58.
4. Go to two different stores with someone in your class and compare the prices of four to six of the same items in each store; for example, dictionary, notebook, pens, desk calendar, calculator, or camera, tripod, film, book on photography, photo album. Together decide which store you'd prefer to shop in. For what reasons, other than price, might you choose one store over another?
5. Go to a store with someone in your class or with an American friend. Compare two products that are similar, such as two car batteries, two fans, two TVs, two bikes, two sweaters, two pairs of shoes, two sets of dishes, etc. Discuss the differences between the products (size, material, features, where they are made, quality, durability, cost, warranty, etc.) and decide which one you would buy. (Your teacher may wish to give you a list of specific items to compare.)
6. Go to a used car lot with your class or with a friend. Look at two cars and compare them. Decide which one you think is a better deal and why.
7. Make a list of five drugstore or grocery store items such as bath soap, toothpaste, deodorant, shampoo, and after-shave lotion or perfume. Then interview two or three Americans and ask them which brand they prefer and why. Present your results to the class.

Notes

Final Activity

Discuss the following questions with your instructor.

1. If you were going to take a vacation, what would you consider before choosing where to go?
2. What kinds of things do you like to do on a vacation?
3. If you were going on vacation with several friends, would you try to convince them to go to a place you liked or would you want to choose a place that everybody would like?

Choosing a Vacation Spot

You and your friends are planning a trip during July or August and want to visit an interesting city in the United States. Your group has chosen four possible places: Seattle, Boston, Las Vegas, and Honolulu. You get together to discuss the advantages and disadvantages of each place. If you have a favorite choice, be sure to tell your reasons to the rest of the group. Then, together make a final decision about where to go. Your instructor will put you in groups of threes or fours. Be prepared to present and explain your decision to the class. Use expressions of comparison and contrast to explain your decision.

Seattle, Washington

Nick Gunderson, Seattle–King County News Bureau

Description: Seattle is located on the Northwest coast. It has almost two million inhabitants. There are many tourist attractions in Seattle's lively downtown area as well as in, around, and outside of the city.

Weather: In July and August daytime temperatures are in the 70s and 80s. There is a relatively small amount of rain during the summer months.

Transportation from the airport: Bus, shuttle, taxi.

City transportation: Good bus transportation; free downtown buses.

Sights inside the city: Take a tour of the Boeing Factory or visit the Museum of Flight. Visit the famous downtown Pike Place Market, the Seattle Art Museum, the Seattle Aquarium, or historic Pioneer Square with its art galleries, bookstores, popular taverns and restaurants. Take a tour and learn more about Seattle: Join a walking tour of Seattle's shopping district, an underground tour of the city, or a kayak tour in the bay along the waterfront. Go to the top of the Space Needle for spectacular 360-degree views of Seattle. See the Seattle Asian Art Museum in Volunteer Park. Plan a night out at the theatre, a concert, or a film. Or, take in a Seattle Mariner's (baseball) game.

Sights nearby: Rent a car and drive to Mount Rainier or Olympic National Park for hiking and beautiful vistas or swim at one of the area's lake parks. Take a boat trip to one of the nearby islands.

Price of hotels: average.

Boston, Massachusetts

Description: Boston is located on Massachusetts Bay on the Atlantic Coast. It is a historic city that played an important role in the American Revolution. Today metropolitan Boston has 3,800,000 inhabitants.

Weather: In July and August daytime temperatures are in the 70s and low 80s with some chance of showers.

Transportation from the airport: Subway (reached by free buses), water shuttle, and taxi.

City transportation: Good subway (the "T") and bus service.

Sights inside the city: Take a walking tour of the historic Freedom Trail and learn about the people and events of the Revolutionary War. Visit New England Aquarium and the Museum of Fine Arts. Watch a Red Sox (baseball) game at Fenway Park. Walk through the Quincy Market and the Italian District or have lunch or dinner in Chinatown. Take the subway to Cambridge and tour Harvard University, the oldest university in the country. Relax or take a paddleboat ride at the Boston Public Garden or take a cruise in Boston Harbor. Bike rental is available. There are 80 miles of bike trails in and around Boston.

Sights nearby: Take a morning or afternoon Whale Watch cruise. Rent a car and drive to Cape Cod or another nearby beach.

Price of hotels: expensive

Las Vegas, Nevada

Las Vegas News Bureau

Description: Nearly 30 million tourists visit Las Vegas yearly to take advantage of its gambling casinos and its liberal marriage and divorce laws. Located in the Southwestern section of the United States, Las Vegas has a population of almost 1,000,000 inhabitants.

Weather: In July and August, there is little rain and low humidity. Daytime temperatures can be hot with highs in the 90s. Nights are cooler.

Transportation from the airport: There are many free hotel buses, inexpensive minibuses, and taxis.

City transportation: Good local bus service is available.

Sights inside the city: Visit luxurious Caesar's Palace casino with its exclusive shops and restaurants. See the Sigfried & Roy magic show or dolphin show at the Mirage. Go to the top of the 1,149 foot Stratosphere Tower, the country's tallest observation tower. Enjoy nightly shows and comic acts at reasonable prices or sometimes free. Take your kids to the MGM Grand amusement park or the Wet 'n Wild Park on the Las Vegas strip. Eat as much as you want at one of the many inexpensive buffets, $5–15. Get married in a hot air balloon.

Sights nearby: Take a day trip to Lake Mead for a cruise, sailing, and fishing; stop for a tour of Hoover Dam, one of the highest dams (760 feet) ever built.

Price of hotels: Mid-week bargains range from $25 to $60.

Honolulu, Hawaii, USS *Arizona* Memorial at Pearl Harbor

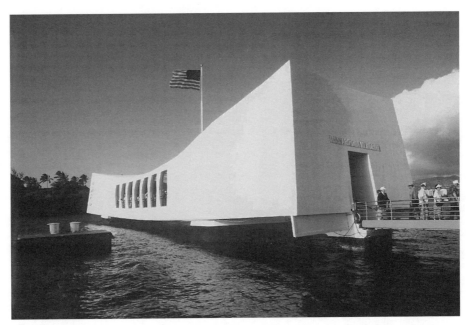

Daniel Martinez, National Park Service

Description: Located on Oahu Island in the Pacific, Honolulu is the state capital of Hawaii. It has a population of 400,000.

Weather: In July and August the daytime temperatures are in the 80s with little rain.

Transportation from the airport: Shuttle to downtown; many hotels have free shuttle service.

City transportation: Inexpensive bus service around the island; bikes and mopeds also available.

Sights inside the city and around the island: View Polynesian and Hawaiian artifacts at the anthropological Bishop Museum. Visit the Waikiki Aquarium, the Hawaii Maritime Center, and the Aloha Tower and shopping mall. Take a walking tour of Honolulu or a stroll in Chinatown. Take a trip to the National Memorial Cemetery of the Pacific overlooking Pearl Harbor and the extinct Diamond Head Volcano. Eat at one of many fine restaurants, enjoy a dinner cruise, go to concerts, the opera, or ballet. Relax at romantic Waikiki Beach, snorkel in Hanauma Bay. Learn to surf, scuba dive, or kayak.

Price of hotels: Average

© Susan M. Reinhart

7

Giving Your Opinion, Agreeing, and Disagreeing

 Warm-up

1. You go to a movie with a friend. Your friend thinks the movie was wonderful and you think it was not very good.

2. A couple you know is expecting a baby and is thinking of naming it Caesar. You don't like the name. What would you say? Would it make a difference if the baby were already named Caesar? If so, why?

3. If you and your friends were sitting around talking about a topic such as international marriages, would you give your opinion? Under what circumstances wouldn't you give your opinion?

4. In which of the above situations is it easiest to give your opinion? Why?

Dialogue for Analysis

A New Retirement Home

Situation: Sandra and David, who are friends, are discussing the advantages and disadvantages of retirement homes.

Sandra: I just read in today's newspaper that they're going to build a new retirement home in town.

David: Why would anyone want to live in a retirement home? Why can't older parents just live with their children?

Sandra: Maybe they don't want to live with their children. In a retirement home, they'd be more independent. They'd have their own apartment. And a lot of children think their parents would be happier in a retirement home. I think it's a good option.

David: But don't you think older people would really get lonely and depressed thinking that their families don't want to look after them, now that they're older.

Sandra: Maybe, but it seems to me that a retirement home is a good place to make new friends and participate in activities like exercise classes, and gardening, and even trips.

David: That may be, but it's not the same as having a real family life and being with people who really care about them.

Sandra: Yes, but if they were living with their children, some older people would end up spending a lot of time at home alone because nowadays everyone works. They might feel less lonely in a retirement home where there are always people around.

David: But you have to remember that older people don't have to be in a retirement home to participate in activities for senior citizens. Our town has a lot of programs for seniors.

Sandra: I agree, but what if . . . .

David: And those retirement home apartments are usually small and expensive.

Sandra: That may be true, but many older people don't want a lot of space. And the rent includes a lot of services there like meals, house cleaning, laundry service, and even some transportation.

David: Well, I just know it would be hard for me to put my parents in a retirement home.

Sandra: I guess every individual's case is different. A retirement home might be just the right place for some people.

Dialogue Analysis

1. How does the topic get introduced?

2. Who has stronger feelings about the topic? How can you tell?

3. Does Sandra think that retirement homes are good for everyone? How about David? Does he think that retirement homes are bad for everyone?

4. Forgetting your own opinion about retirement homes, who do you think is a more persuasive speaker? Why?

5. What are some expressions Sandra and David use to disagree with each other? Do any of these seem inappropriate or offensive?

6. What do you think Sandra was about to say when she began with "I agree, but what if . . . ?"

7. Do you think Sandra gets offended that David interrupts her?

8. What's your own opinion about retirement homes?

Expressions Used in Giving Your Opinion

1. I think . . . .
2. But don't you think . . . ?
3. It seems to me that . . . .
4. That may be (true), but . . . .
5. Yes, but . . . .
6. I see your point, but . . . .
7. I agree but . . . .
8. But what if . . . .
9. Yes, I guess . . . .
10. But you have to remember . . . .

Points to Remember

1. People's opinions on a given topic differ. It is interesting to discuss a topic with someone and share opinions. However, sharing opinions does not necessarily mean coming to an agreement or convincing someone you are right. The conversation may end after the participants have stated their opinions and further discussion doesn't appear fruitful.

2. Expressions that show partial agreement such as "Yes, but . . . ," "I agree, but . . . ," and "I see your point, but . . . " are less direct than expressions that show total disagreement such as "I completely disagree," "You're wrong," "That's ridiculous," and "That's a stupid idea." The latter expressions are much stronger and could be considered inappropriate or impolite in some social settings, especially in which the participants do not know each other well.

3. When discussing a controversial subject, one speaker may interrupt the other from time to time. However, if a speaker is interrupted too many times, he/she may feel his/her opinion isn't being heard.

4. A person may not wish to offer an opinion in certain situations because it could insult the listener no matter how it is stated.

5. In unit 6, "Making Choices—Comparing and Contrasting" the speakers were generally trying to make decisions together. They used comparison and contrast as one way of evaluating possible choices. However, it is sometimes difficult for two people to come to a decision together when they disagree. Compromises or other alternatives may be necessary.

Class and Small Group Activity

Together with your teacher discuss and write down some of the pros and cons of the following topic:

Foreign students should be allowed to work while they are studying in the United States.

Pros	Cons
1.	1.
2.	2.
3.	3.
4.	4.

Give your personal opinion about this subject to your partner and find out your partner's opinion. Use appropriate expressions for giving your opinion.

Next, in small groups, choose a topic from the list on page 74 and discuss it. With your partners, write down some of the pros and cons. Then present your topic to the class with the pros and cons your group has discussed and ask members of the class to contribute their opinion. Or, your instructor may ask your group to informally debate one of the topics. In a small group of four, set up the debate using one of these topics. In pairs, prepare one side of the argument. Then debate the topic with the two people who have prepared the opposite side of the argument. Respond to the arguments of your opponents with counterarguments. Use expressions from this lesson to state your opinion. Your instructor may ask your group to debate the topic in front of the entire class.

Topics:
- Teachers should receive high salaries for the jobs they perform.
- Taxes on cigarettes should be high.
- Tourism destroys a country.
- Once a person is married, he/she should stay married.
- Computers bring people closer together.
- Children can learn a lot from watching TV.

Topic:

Pros	Cons
1.	1.
2.	2.
3.	3.
4.	4.

Class and Small Group Activity

Discuss the following questions with your instructor:

1. Do you know anyone who wanted to marry someone his/her parents didn't approve of? What were the circumstances? What happened?
2. What are some reasons why parents might not want their son or daughter to marry a certain person?
3. Do you think it's important to marry someone your parents like?

Your teacher will put you in small groups. Together read the following story. Your instructor will help you with any vocabulary you do not understand. Then discuss the story and the questions in the group discussion section.

Marriage and Parents

Abe is a 25-year-old foreign student. He has been in the United States about two years now and is just finishing up his master's degree in engineering. For over a year he has been dating an American, Debby. Debby is 24 and is also an engineer. They really get along well and have started making plans to get married. Abe would like to stay in the United States since Debby doesn't speak his language well and job opportunities for them both are better in the United States. They both know that there will be a lot of problems and adjustments for them both since they not only come from different cultures but also from different religions. To make the adjustments a little easier, Debby has been doing a lot of reading about Abe's country and has been learning his language. Abe has mentioned Debby in his letters to his parents, but he has never mentioned marriage. Since they will be in the United States for his graduation, he writes them a letter explaining his intention to marry Debby and live in the States.

Debby is a little apprehensive about meeting Abe's parents. To make things worse, Abe has to take a final exam the day his parents arrive. So Debby goes alone to meet them at the airport and takes them to their hotel room. They are rather quiet but polite. They both speak English fairly well, but they don't ask Debby any questions about her and Abe. When Abe's parents have gotten settled into their hotel room and Debby is about to leave, Abe's parents turn to her. Abe's father speaks, "We are glad that you are here alone because we want to be frank with you. We do not want you to marry our son. We know it will never work. We want Abe to marry someone from his own culture and live in his own country near his family. We will do anything we can to prevent the marriage." Debby doesn't say anything. She leaves the hotel room and goes home. Later Abe stops over to see her. She tells him what happened between her and his parents.

Questions for Group Discussion

1. Now that Abe knows how his parents feel, what do you think he will do?
2. Do you think Abe's parents dislike Debby personally? What do you think are the reasons why his parents don't want Debby and Abe to get married?
3. How could Abe's parents try to prevent the marriage? Do you think it would be different if their daughter were marrying an American man?
4. If Debby and Abe decide to get married, do you think the marriage will last? Why or why not? Mention some advantages and disadvantages of their situation.
5. When two people from different countries get married, what do you think is their biggest problem—their culture, their religion, their family, their level of education, or something else?
6. Would you marry someone your parents didn't approve of? What do you think Abe should do now?

After discussing the preceding questions, choose two people from your group to role-play the following scene:

> Abe and his father are talking. They are both presenting their sides of the argument. Abe is telling his father why he thinks a marriage between himself and Debby would work. His father takes the opposite view.

Be prepared to present your role-play to the class. How does Abe try to convince his father that marrying Debby is a good idea? What arguments does his father use to try to convince Abe that it is not. What expressions do they use to give their opinion?

Community Activity

Elicit the opinion of an American on the following questions. Take notes and be prepared to present the opinion to the class.

1. Do you think a marriage between two people of different nationalities can work? Why or why not? What do you think would be the biggest problems?

2. If a father doesn't consent to his daughter's marriage, should she get married anyway? Why or why not? What if it were his son?

Write down expressions that the American you asked used to express his or her opinion.

Final Activity

1. Read the following situation with your teacher. Your teacher will explain any new vocabulary you're having difficulty with.

Should Mothers Work?

Barbara Sanders is a wife and the mother of two children, ages two-and-a-half and four. Her husband, Tom, is a businessman and makes an excellent salary. Before Barbara had children, she worked as an architect for the government, designing low-income housing. She quit her job when she became pregnant but is now interested in returning to work. She has recently been offered another good position in the government.

Her husband feels it is unnecessary for her to work since the family does not need the added income. He also thinks that a woman should stay home with her children. If Barbara feels the need to do socially important work, he thinks that she should do volunteer work one or two days a week.

Barbara, on the other hand, has missed the excitement of her profession and doesn't feel she'd be satisfied doing volunteer work. She would also prefer to have her own income and not depend on her husband for money. She doesn't think it's necessary to stay home every day with the children, and she knows a very reliable day-care center that could take both children. The staff is very well trained and the program has both social and educational components. She thinks that after an initial adjustment, her children will enjoy being in day care. Tom doesn't think a day-care worker can replace a mother and thinks it's a bad idea for children to spend so much time away from their mother, especially since they are so young.

2. Your instructor will group you with two or three other students and select a student leader. Together reread the situation and make a summary of the husband's and wife's opinions.

Husband's Opinions
Example: Barbara shouldn't work because we don't need the money.

1.

2.

3.

4.

Wife's Opinion

1.

2.

3.

4.

3. Now discuss the problem together. Give your opinions. Use appropriate expressions you have learned for giving opinions. Respond to others' opinions as much as possible.

4. Answer the following questions with your group.
   a. Did everyone in your group offer an opinion?
   b. Did you feel that you and/or others in your group expressed their opinions appropriately or inappropriately? Give examples.
   c. Do you think that your opinion was altered after you listened to the arguments of others in your group?
5. Summarize your final opinion on the subject. Present it to the class.

Notes

© José Sánchez-H.

8

Offers of Help and Requests for Help

Part One: Offers of Help

 Warm-up

1. What would you say to your instructor if you saw her carrying a large pile of books down the hall and you wanted to offer to help?

2. Why might an instructor turn down (refuse) your offer of help?

3. Why do people sometimes refuse a first offer of help but accept a second offer?

Dialogues for Analysis A

Situation: Ms. Ames, an instructor, is moving some video equipment down the hall. A student of hers, Daniel, offers her help.

Dialogue 1

Daniel: Can I help you?
Ms. Ames: Thanks.

Dialogue 2

Daniel: Would you like some help?
Ms. Ames: I'm all right, thanks.
Daniel: Really, I'm going that way.
Ms. Ames: OK. Thanks.

Dialogue 3

Daniel: Do you want some help with that equipment?
Ms. Ames: I've got it, thanks.
Daniel: You sure?
Ms. Ames: Yeah. Thanks, anyway.

Dialogue Analysis

1. In dialogue 1, the student offered help by saying, "Can I help you?" "May I help you?" would *not* be used here. When do people say "May I help you?"

2. What does "Thanks" mean in dialogue 1?

3. In dialogue 2, what does the instructor mean when she says, "I'm all right, thanks"?

4. Why does the student say "really"?

5. Why do you think the instructor accepted the student's second offer of help?

6. In dialogue 3, do you think the instructor is sincere about not wanting help? How can you tell?

7. Why isn't "No, thanks" an appropriate way of refusing help in this situation?

Dialogues for Analysis B

Situation: John and Vicky are friends from school. John is studying chemistry and is having a lot of problems. He has a big exam tomorrow and is afraid he might fail. He sees Vicky, who is a chemistry major, in the library and goes over to talk to her. He has his chemistry book in his hand.

Dialogue 1

John: I'm really worried about my chemistry exam tomorrow.
Vicky: Want me to help you?
John: Really?
Vicky: I'm serious. I'd be glad to help.
John: I'd really appreciate it.

Dialogue 2

John: I'm really worried about my chemistry exam tomorrow.
Vicky: Well, I've got some homework to finish up, but I could probably help you for a little while.
John: That's OK, Vicky. I think I can manage. But, thanks anyway.

Dialogue 3

John: I'm really worried about my chemistry exam tomorrow.
Vicky: I'd really like to help but I've got to work till midnight. Maybe Andrea's got time. She's a chem major.
John: Good idea. Maybe I'll give her a call. Thanks.

Dialogue Analysis

1. Does John directly ask Vicky for help in any of the 3 dialogues?

2. Compare Vicky's offer of help in dialogues 1 and 2. In which dialogue(s) is her offer more emphatic (stronger)? What strategy does she use to make a less emphatic offer?

3. In dialogue 1, why do you think John doesn't accept Vicky's offer immediately?

4. Why does Vicky feel it is necessary to say, "I'm serious. I'd be glad to help."

5. How does John respond to Vicky's hesitant offer in dialogue 2? What does his response show?

6. What expression does Vicky use in dialogue 3 to show that she cannot help? Why does she recommend someone else?

7. How might John have directly asked Vicky for help?

Points to Remember

1. If someone offers help, it is generally viewed as a commitment. If a person cannot give help, he/she usually doesn't make such an offer or states that he/she cannot give help. Sometimes an excuse or reason is given.
2. Sometimes people offer help with some hesitancy, such as "I could help you for a little while but have an appointment in an hour." Whether or not to accept a hesitant offer of help may depend on how much the help is needed.
3. Sometimes we turn down an offer of help in order not to inconvenience the offerer. A person may offer help twice in order to show a sincere desire to help. If an offer is turned down twice, it generally means that the person genuinely does not want help.
4. "May I help you?" is used by people who work in stores, offices, schools, or other types of business. "Can I help you?" "Do you want me to help you" "Would you like some help?" and "Do you need help?" are more general offers of help.
5. Depending on the significance of help offered, expressions of appreciation may vary from a casual "Thanks" or "Thanks a lot" to a more formal "Thank you. I really appreciate this (it, your help)".
6. "No, thank you" is sometimes not considered a polite way to turn down an offer of help because it is too abrupt. It is used to turn down an offer of food, however. To refuse an offer of help, the speaker may use such expressions as "Thanks a lot, but . . . .", "That's OK (all right). Thanks anyway," or "I'm OK (all right). Thanks."

Class Activity (to be done by the class as a whole)

Discuss the following situations with your teacher.

1. Your neighbors are going on vacation for two weeks. You offer to check their mail and water the plants. What would be an appropriate offer of help? If your neighbors needed help, how would they respond?

2. You've just had dinner at the house of some American friends. You want to offer to help with the dishes. What could you say? Your friends refuse the offer. What might they say?

3. It's raining, and a friend offers you a ride home from work. What might she say? You turn down the offer because another friend is going to pick you up. How could you politely turn down the offer?

Class Activity (work in pairs or groups of three)

Discuss the following situations with your partner(s). Practice what you would say, and share your dialogue with the class.

1. A friend drops by to visit you one evening. The weather outside turns cool and the friend appears to be cold. You offer to lend her a sweater and she accepts.

2. You see a friend who is changing a flat tire. You make a hesitant offer to help, because you are going to meet someone for dinner and have good clothes on. Your friend sees that you are dressed up and refuses the offer.

3. Your friend is looking for something on the ground. You offer to help, but your friend says she lost her contact lens and is sure she can find it. You offer again and this time she accepts.

Homework Activity

Read the following situations and write dialogues that include an appropriate offer to help. Be prepared to present your dialogues to the class.

1. Your roommate is carrying two heavy bags of groceries. Offer to take one. Your roommate rejects your offer. You offer again.

You:

_____

Your roommate:

_____

You:

_____

Your roommate:

_____

2. You are working at the information desk in a dormitory. Offer to help a new student who seems to be looking for something. It turns out that the student is looking for the mailboxes.

You:

_____

New Student:

_____

3. Your friend indicates he needs a ride to the shopping mall. Unfortunately you have a big exam to study for. Very hesitantly offer him a ride.

Friend:

_____

You:

_____

Friend:

_____

Part Two: Requests for Help

 ## Warm-up

1. How would you ask a friend to lend you money for a phone call?

2. If you were sick and needed a friend to go shopping for you, would you ask for help in the same way? Why or why not?

3. Would you ask a stranger to lend you money for a phone call in the same way you would ask a friend? What would you say?

Dialogues for Analysis

Dialogue 1

Situation: Mark is coming into his apartment with two bags of groceries in his arms. His roommate is standing near the door.

Mark:	Hey, Dan, get the door, OK?
Roommate:	Sure. It looks like you bought enough groceries for a month.

Dialogue 2

Situation: Mark is coming into his apartment building with a load of groceries. He asks a stranger for help.

Mark:	Excuse me, would you mind opening the door for me?
Stranger:	Sure.
Mark:	Thanks.

Dialogue 3

Situation: Mark is at a party and needs a ride home. He asks his friend, Debby.

Mark:	When are you leaving the party, Debby?
Debby:	In about an hour.
Mark:	Could you give me a ride home?
Debby:	Sure. It's right on the way.
Mark:	Thanks.

Dialogue 4

Situation: Mark wants to go to his cousin's wedding but doesn't have a car. He's talking to his friend, Debby.

Mark:	Debby, I want to ask you a big favor. I was wondering if I could borrow your car Saturday afternoon. I have to go to my cousin's wedding and it's twenty miles from here.
Debby:	I'd really like to help you out but Saturday I'm driving some friends of mine to the lake. Otherwise, you could use it.
Mark:	Well, thanks, anyway.
Debby:	You know, maybe you could rent a car. That place downtown isn't very expensive.
Mark:	That's a good idea. I'll check into it.

Dialogue Analysis

1. In dialogue 1, how does Mark request help? Why is it probably all right for Mark to use an imperative form plus the tag like "OK" or "would you (ya')?"

2. In dialogue 2, Mark is making the same request. Why do you think he uses a different form?

3. Compare dialogues 1 and 3. Why doesn't Mark use the same form in both cases? What's different about the two requests?

4. Do you think Mark's request in dialogue 4 is more or less formal than in dialogues 1–3? Why?

5. In dialogue 4, what if Debby wasn't using her car on Saturday but didn't want to lend Mark her car? What could she say?

Expressions Used in Making Requests for Help

This list is loosely ordered from informal to formal. The formality of a request for help is influenced by the difficulty of the task as perceived by the person asking for help and the relationship of the participants. Notice that "please" is generally not used when making a request for help.

1. Get the door, OK (or would you)?
2. How about carrying this for me?
3. Do me a favor and lend me your dictionary for a minute.
4. Would you lend me a dime?
5. Do you have a pen I could borrow?
6. Can you help me take the garbage?
7. Do you have time to explain this math problem to me?
8. Could you give me a ride home?
9. Would you mind helping me look for my ring?
10. Do you think you could help me study for my exam?
11. Would you be willing to take care of my cat while I'm in Florida?
12. I hate to ask you this, but would you be able to drive me to school? My car won't start.
13. I was wondering if you would mind helping me fill out a job application.
14. I have a big favor to ask you. My car is at the garage and I was wondering if you would have time today to drive me over there.

▶ Points to Remember

1. We make more formal requests when we consider the request to be an imposition. For example, "How about lending me a dime?" would be much less of an imposition than "I was wondering if you could lend me $100." The formality of a request also depends on the relationship between the people involved.

2. In English, "please" is not generally used when making a request for help. To make a request sound more polite or formal, other expressions such as "could you," "would you mind," and "I was wondering if you could" are used instead.

3. A request is often accompanied by an explanation, especially if the reason for the request is not obvious to the hearer, as in "Could I borrow your telephone for a minute? I locked myself out of the house and have to call my wife."

4. Expressions like "I wish I could help, but . . . " and "I'd really like to help you, but . . . " are used to politely turn down a request for help. The speaker may accompany the refusal with an excuse.

5. We can request help indirectly by stating a need or desire, as in "Oh, I'm really having trouble typing this paper. I don't think I'll get done on time." However, the hearer then may have the option of recognizing the statement as a request or simply as a statement of fact. A request for a large amount of money or an expensive belonging, such as a car, may not be welcomed. An indirect request for help may be more appropriate than a direct one because it might put the listener in a less awkward position.

Class Activity (work in pairs)

Look at the following incomplete dialogues. Complete each dialogue with an appropriate request. Consider both your relationship to the person and the request you are making. Explain to the class why you chose the form you did. Then, ask your instructor which request form he/she would use.

Request 1: Borrow a piece of paper from a classmate you don't know at all.

You: _____

_____

Classmate: Sure. Is one enough?

Request 2: Ask a good friend for help finding a number in the telephone book.

You: _____

_____

Roommate: Sure. Where are you calling?

Request 3: Ask a teacher to help you with a job application.

You: _____

_____

Teacher: I'd be glad to help you, but I'm busy today until 4:00.

Request 4: Ask a neighbor you don't know well if you can borrow a hammer.

You: _____

_____

Neighbor: Sure. Just a minute. I'll get it.

Request 5: Ask a stranger to take a photograph of you and a friend at the city fountain.

You: _____

_____

Stranger: I'd be glad to.

Homework Activity

Write dialogues for two of the situations on page 92. Make sure the request form you choose is appropriate. Hand in your dialogues for comments from your instructor.

Situation 1: You ask your English instructor to correct the grammar on your job application. You realize that this will take a long time and is not part of your instructor's job. The instructor is willing to do it but won't have time for the next few days.

Situation 2: You need some help learning to use the spell check on your computer. Ask a friend for help.

Situation 3: You have just come to the U.S. and want to open a bank account but don't know how. You've only made one American friend so far. Tell your American friend about your problem, hoping that he/she will offer to help you. When your friend offers help, accept the offer.

Community Activity

Interview an American and write down his/her responses. In class discuss the responses with your group or with the class as a whole. When you get to item 3, tell other class members what you would say in your own country and how it is similar or different from the American's response.

1. In which of the following situations would you say "May I help you?" Otherwise, how would you offer help?
   a. You're working at a café and a customer enters.

   b. Your friend expresses frustration at not knowing how to get on the internet.

   c. You see a stranger walking in front of you trip and fall to the ground.

   d. You are working as a library assistant and someone comes to the desk to ask where the restroom is.

2. How would you make a request for help in the following circumstances? What would you say?
   a. You need to borrow $5 from your brother or sister until you can get to the bank.

   b. You were sick and missed class. You don't know any students in the class very well. You ask one student if you can photocopy her notes.

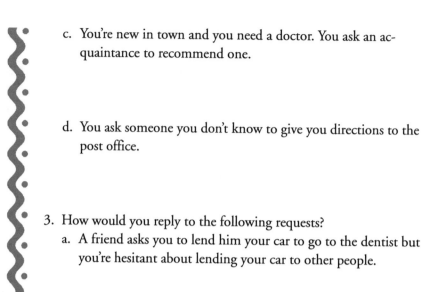

c. You're new in town and you need a doctor. You ask an acquaintance to recommend one.

d. You ask someone you don't know to give you directions to the post office.

3. How would you reply to the following requests?
   a. A friend asks you to lend him your car to go to the dentist but you're hesitant about lending your car to other people.

   b. Your friend is coming to visit from out of town. He calls you to pick him up at the train station at 2:00. You have a class from 2:00 to 4:00.

   c. A neighbor wants to borrow a CD from you. She has another CD of yours already but hasn't returned it.

 Final Activity (role-play in pairs)

Your teacher will group you with one other student and assign one of the following role-plays for you to prepare. First, discuss the role-play with your partner, then practice what you would say in this situation. Be prepared to perform the role-play in front of the class. The teacher and the other students will discuss and compare each role-play presented and make comments on how it can be improved.

Situation 1: You met your next-door neighbor but you aren't well acquainted yet. You need a hammer to hang some pictures. You ask your neighbor, even though you're a little embarrassed about asking someone you don't know very well for a favor. Your neighbor wouldn't mind lending the hammer but doesn't have one.

Situation 2: You injured your knee and can't walk without crutches. You can't drive because it's painful for you to step on the accelerator or the brake. You need to get to the university to take an exam. Your friend from class has a car, but you know he is busy studying for exams and you feel bad about asking him to take the time to drive you to the university. But you are desperate. Your friend is willing because it turns out he has an exam at the same time.

Situation 3: You would like to go to Boston for a conference but don't have money to stay in a hotel. Your good friend has a small apartment in Boston. Your friend has already invited you to come and visit so you don't think he/she will mind if you stay there. You call up to find out.

© José Sánchez-H.

9

Getting and Giving Advice

 Warm-up

1. If you wanted to paint your room and had never done any painting before, what would you do before you started?

2. If you were having trouble with your English, would you get advice from someone? If so, would you prefer to talk about the problem with a friend or a teacher?

Dialogues for Analysis

Situation: Li, a Taiwanese student is having problems learning English. He goes to a friend, Franz, who is good at English and asks for advice. Franz gives him advice and recommends that he also speak to the teacher, Ms. Benson.

Learning English

Dialogue 1

Li: It's so hard for me to learn English. Why is it so easy for you?

Franz: I didn't know you were having problems. Maybe it's easier for me because I already speak two other languages. But also, I really have to work at it.

Li: Well, I always do my homework and go to class. What else do you think would help?

Franz: Do you read the local newspaper?

Li: No.

Franz: Well, you might try reading the newspaper. You can learn a lot of vocabulary that way and it gives you things to talk about with Americans. I always talk to Americans when I get a chance, though sometimes it's hard.

Li: But, how do you meet Americans? I only know other foreign students.

Franz: How about joining the International Club or sitting with an American in the cafeteria. I sometimes do that.

Li: Those are good ideas, but I'm embarrassed to speak English.

Franz: I was that way too, but you'll get over it if you keep trying. Why don't you talk to your English teacher. She might have some suggestions.

Li: Maybe I will. Thanks for your advice.

Dialogue Analysis

1. How does Li introduce his problem?

2. Why does Li say, "I always do my homework and go to class"?

3. How does Li ask for advice?

4. What advice forms does Franz use when he gives advice?

5. Why do you think the use of "must" is generally inappropriate for giving advice, such as, "You must read the newspaper every day"?

6. Do you think it would be easy to ask someone like Franz for advice? Why?

Dialogue 2 (later in the day)

Li: Excuse me, Ms. Benson. Can I talk to you for a minute?

Ms. Benson: Sure, Li. How can I help you?

Li: I'm really having problems learning English. I do all my work and come to class, but I'm not making much progress. What do you think I should do?

Ms. Benson: Maybe it's a little hard for you to learn English, but you **are** improving. Do you spend much time with Americans?

Li: No, not really.

Ms. Benson: Maybe you could get a conversation partner through the International Center. Another thing I'd recommend is not waiting for Americans to invite you somewhere. There's nothing wrong with calling up someone you've met and asking them to go somewhere.

Li: Those are good ideas. Is there anything else I should do?

Ms. Benson: Go to English-speaking movies, watch television, and get in the habit of reading the newspaper every day.

Li: That'll help, I think.

Ms. Benson: If you really still feel you're not making progress, I suggest you get a private tutor a few hours a week.

Li: Yeah. I might do that. Thanks for your suggestions.

Dialogue Analysis

1. What does Ms. Benson say that shows she's willing to help Li?

2. How does Li ask for advice?

3. What does Ms. Benson say to Li to make him feel better?

4. What information does Ms. Benson try to get from Li before giving advice?

5. Are Ms. Benson's ways of giving advice very different from those Franz used?

6. Ms. Benson uses the advice forms, "I'd recommend . . . " and "I suggest . . . " Why do you think these would be inappropriate for Franz to use?

7. Ms. Benson uses the imperative (command) form. How does she use it? Is Ms. Benson ordering Li to do something?

8. Was it helpful for Li to get advice from more than one person? Why or why not?

Advice Forms from the Dialogues

Getting Advice

How do you . . . ?
What would you do?
What do you think I should (ought to) do?
What do you think would help?
Is there anything else I could (should) do?
What would you recommend?

Giving Advice

You might try . . .
I sometimes . . .
How about (V + *-ing*)
Have you ever thought of (V + *-ing*)
Why don't you . . .
(Maybe) You could (should) . . .
It might be a good idea to . . .
I guess I would . . .
I think you could (should) . . .
If I were you, I'd . . .
I suggest (recommend) (V + *-ing* or *you* + infinitive)
Another thing I'd recommend is (V + *-ing* or *that you* + infinitive)

Points to Remember

1. Giving advice is not comparable to telling someone what to do. When giving advice, Americans generally avoid forms such as "You must . . " or "You have to . . . ". Suggestion expressions such as "You might (could) . . .", "How about . . . ?", and "Why don't you . . . ?" are both common and appropriate. "Should" is also used when giving advice but may be considered stronger than "might" or "could." The imperative form (see dialogue 2) may sometimes be used appropriately to give advice and in these situations should not usually be taken as a command.

2. The advice forms "I'd recommend . . . " and "I suggest" are more formal than the other forms listed on this page and are generally used by professionals, such as doctors, business consultants, counselors, and instructors when giving advice to their clients or students.

Class Activity (to be done by the class as a whole)

The following story is about a student named Mia. Mia has a problem and is seeking advice from friends in the class. Choose one student in the class to be Mia. She will explain her problem and ask for advice, using one or two of the forms for getting advice from the list. Give her advice, using some of the advice forms for giving advice in the list. Your instructor will write down the forms so that the class as a whole can later discuss and evaluate them. Your instructor may ask you to do this activity in small groups of four or five students. If so, one person in your group can be Mia and another can be in charge of writing down the advice forms.

Situation:
Mia is studying in the United States. She has one more year to go before she graduates. She has just received news from her parents that there is a financial crisis in her country and that they are no longer going to be able to send her as much money as before. Mia knows that it's very important for her to cut down on her expenses. Right now she has a car and a spacious two-bedroom apartment near campus that she shares with one other person. She doesn't work and has so far depended on her family for all her spending money. She doesn't buy a lot of clothes but her books are expensive and she likes to buy a couple of CDs every month. She also goes out with friends to a restaurant, concert, or to the movies once in a while as a break from studying. She was just beginning to plan a trip to the Grand Canyon with some friends during the summer break. She needs a pair of new glasses and two tires for her car. She also was hoping to buy a faster printer for her computer.

Notes

Class Activity (role-play in pairs or groups of three)

Your teacher will group you with one or two other students and assign one of the following discussion topics. One member of the group will take the role of the person asking for help. The other(s) will offer advice. Before beginning the discussion, read the problem and think about what you will say. Use appropriate advice forms when asking for and giving advice. After you finish your discussion, your instructor may ask those who gave advice to repeat their advice for the entire class using common advice forms.

1. You have been smoking for about 6 years now. You've started getting more colds and tiring more easily, especially when you play sports. You know that smoking isn't good for your health and you want to stop. You tried to stop once but couldn't. One problem is that some of your friends smoke. Ask a friend (or friends) for advice.

2. You use the computer a lot, maybe 4 or 5 hours a day. You've started getting headaches, neck pain, and backaches. When you don't use your computer, you feel better but you need it for your work and like to spend time keeping in touch with friends on e-mail, surfing the Web, and playing video games. Ask a friend (or friends) for advice.

3. You're thinking about buying a car because winter is coming and you're tired of walking in cold weather. You've never had a car and don't know if it would be a good idea to get one or not. Also, if you get one, you don't know what kind to get or whether to get a new or used car. Ask a friend (or friends) for advice.

4. You have just received news that family members are coming to visit you. You hope to show them a good time. You want to plan some things to do either in the town you're living in or nearby. You ask a friend for advice.

Notes

Community Activity

Do one of the following activities outside of class. Bring the information to class for discussion. Where appropriate, compare the American's answers with responses of class members.

1. Interview an American and ask the American what advice he/she would give you in one of the following situations.
   a. A family member of yours is coming to visit you from your country. Where would the American suggest you take your visitor and/or what things would he/she suggest you do?
   b. You are interested in buying a car. What tips would the American give you on buying a car in the U.S.?
2. Contact the American Cancer Association or a similar organization to get advice on how to quit smoking. Be prepared to share the advice with the class, perhaps in a role-play.
3. Interview an American to find out the names of three or four organizations in the community that give advice and the type of advice they give. Bring the list to class.
4. Cut out an advice column from the local newspaper and bring it to class. Discuss one of the letters and tell why you agree or disagree with the advice given.

Class Activity (small group discussion)

Your teacher will group you with two or three other students and assign or have you select one or more of the following letters for you to answer. Each letter is asking for specific advice and is typical of the type of letter found in advice columns in the newspaper. Read the letter over with your group. If you have any trouble understanding it, ask your teacher for help. Then, discuss the letter with your group and try to decide what advice to give. Use appropriate advice forms, changing *you* to *he/she,* as in "Maybe she could . . .", "He might try . . .", "I think she should . . .". Present some of your suggestions to the class. Your instructor will give you feedback on the way in which you gave advice. Your instructor may ask you to write your advice.

Letter 1

Dear Henrietta,

I feel really inadequate because I don't know how to use computers very well, but all my friends seem to be able to use them. I really want to learn how but maybe I just don't feel comfortable around machines. I have access to a nice computer but hardly ever use it, even though it would come in handy sometimes. Can you give me some advice?

Living in the Past

Letter 2

Dear Henrietta,

I have a husband who doesn't do his share of the work. I have a full-time job and study in the evenings two nights a week. When I come home, I'm tired. I usually do the cooking and sometimes end up washing the dishes too. Even though we have agreed to share the cleaning, I do most of it or it doesn't really get done. My husband claims that he doesn't like to cook and doesn't really know how to clean very well because someone else always did the cleaning for his family. The worst thing is that my husband only works half time and spends the rest of the day lying around listening to music or watching TV.

Fed up

Letter 3

Dear Henrietta,

I've been living in the United States for about 6 months. Since I came here I've gained almost 15 pounds and can't even fit into some of my clothes. I don't think people should worry excessively about their weight, but also don't think it's good to gain so much weight. One of the problems is that I've been eating a lot of fast food like cheeseburgers and french fries. I've discovered I love American food like ice cream with chocolate sauce, coffee with whipped cream, and sweet rolls, which I never have in my own country. And here the portions are so much larger than in my own country. I need your advice fast.

Bulging

Letter 4

My wife and I are living in the U.S. with our son and daughter, who are teenagers. They are attending public high school, and we are worried because we think that they may be getting into drugs. They come home late from school, don't tell us where they went, don't take their studies seriously any more, and sometimes don't even obey us. They have some friends we don't approve of. We talk to them but they don't seem to listen. Lately, we are beginning to suspect that they are stealing money from us, maybe to buy drugs. Kids don't get into this kind of trouble in our country. We're worried. We don't want our kids to end up in a juvenile home or in prison. What can we do?

Desperate

Notes

Homework and Final Activity

At home write a letter to Henrietta asking for advice about a real or imaginary problem. If possible, avoid asking for advice on a topic already discussed.

Dear Henrietta,

In class your teacher will put you in groups of threes or fours. Read your letter to your group and ask them for advice. Write an answer to your own letter or someone else's letter using the best pieces of advice from your group. Use appropriate advice forms in your response.

Dear

Henrietta